Perspectives of Continuing Education Programme

Perspectives of Continuing Education Programme

By

Dr. G. Surendra

SONALI PUBLICATIONS
NEW DELHI

First Published–2005
Reprint 2007

ISBN 81-88836-90-7

Published by:

SONALI PUBLICATIONS

4228/1, Ansari Road, Darya Ganj
New Delhi–110 002 (India)
Phone: 23266109, 23279245, • *Fax:* 91-11-23253475

Printed at:
Amit Enterprises

Dedicated
to my
Beloved Parents

PREFACE

After the implementation of Total Literacy and Post-Literacy Campaigns, the Government of India has initiated Continuing Education Programme with review to strengthen and further the basic literacy skills acquired by neo-literates. Continuing Education Centres organised at the grassroot level are manned by preraks. The functions of preraks are wide and varied. The implementation of the programme requires adequate support from the beneficiaries, community and others at large. Research has to play a major role in identifying the strengths and weaknesses of the programme and in suggesting suitable strategies for the smooth functioning of the programme. The present evaluative study on the functioning of Continuing Education Centres in Nellore District (A.P.) is ardent effort in this direction. The study tries to identify the problems of continuing education centres with special reference to preraks and neo-literates, the performances of the preraks and neo-literates and to assess the community opinion towards the functioning of Continuing Education Centres. The study offers workable suggestions towards solving the different problems of the centres and to evaluate the performance of preraks and neo-literates. The first chapter is concerned with introduction; the second chapter is devoted to review of related literature, the third chapter deals with statement of the problem, while the fourth chapter concentrates on method of investigation. The fifth chapter presents results and discussion in clear-cut manner and the last chapter provides a crisp summary of the investigation, conclusions and suggestions. The study is of immense help in improving the status of Continuing Education Programme under National Literacy Mission.

ACKNOWLEDGEMENTS

I acknowledge with a deep sense of gratitude, the inspiring guidance of my Research Supervisor, *Dr. K. Sudha Rani,* Associate Professor, Department of Adult Education, Sri Venkateswara University, Tirupati. Her constant encouragement and initiation at every stage of my research deserves a special mention.

Equally, I am highly beholden to *Prof. G. Prakash Reddy* (Retd.), Department of Anthropology, *Dr. T. Kumara Swamy,* Assistant Director, Department of Adult Education, Sri Venkateswara University, Tirupati for their invaluable suggestions, thought provoking advice and paternal affection.

I am profoundly indebted to *Dr. V. Narayana Reddy,* Associate Professor, Department of Anthropology, Sri Venkateswara University, Tirupati, *Dr. S. Vijaya Kumar,* Fellow, C.S.D., Hyderabad and *Dr. S. Samiullah,* Associate Professor, Department of Psychology for their inspiring guidance, never failing kindness and encouragement which contributed to the successful accomplishment of this thesis.

My heartfelt thanks to my family members and friends who have given me constant support and encouragement in the completion of my work.

Finally, I appreciate very much the patience with which *Mr. D. Murali Krishna,* Computer Operator, *Lakshmi University Xerox,* Tirupati, without whose services, the thesis would not have been completed.

Dr. G. Surendra

Contents

1

INTRODUCTION

Basic education and literacy have been major concerns in several developing countries because literacy is the foundation of human capital for a better quality of life and the very wealth of the nation reflecting in its economic, political and social development. Research has shown that in order to bring about social transformation, literacy must be embedded in social and cultural practices. Literacy and grassroots democratic participation mutually reinforce each other, together they enable people and communities influence the factors that affect their lives.

Literacy, an important tool for communication, learning and information is a virtual precondition for an individual's evolution and national development. Research studies on human cognitive development have established that literacy enhances the critical faculties of an individual and enables to reflect on the existential reality in which they have been placed. It promotes a sense of history and helps combine individuality with universalisation. In this sense, literacy can be regarded as an inalienable fundamental right.

Post-independence India inherited a system of education which was characterised by large scale inter and intra-regional imbalances. The system educated a select few, leaving overwhelming majority in dark creating a large hiatus between the educated and the illiterate. The country's literacy rate in 1947 was only 14 per cent and female literacy was abysmally low at 8 per cent. Educational inequality was aggravated by economic inequality, gender disparity and rigid social stratification.

Eradication of illiteracy has been one of the major national concerns of the Government of India since independence. The need for literate population and universal education for all children in the age group 6-14 years was recognised as a crucial input for nation building and was given due consideration in the Constitution as well as in the successive five year plans. A number of significant programmes have been taken up since independence to eradicate illiteracy among adults. Some of the important programmes along with their salient features are:

SOCIAL EDUCATION

The main elements were literacy, extension, general education, leadership training and social consciousness. The programme was implemented in the First Five Year Plan (1951-56).

GRAM SHIKSHAN MOHIM

Movement for literacy in the rural areas began in 1959 in Satara district of Maharashtra and was later extended to other parts of the state. The programme aimed at imparting basic literacy skills with in a period of four months. By 1963, it spread to all the districts of the state. The programme, however, suffered lack of systematic follow-up and consequently, relapse to illiteracy was massive. The strengths and weaknesses of the programmes were taken as the basis in designing the further programmes.

FARMERS' FUNCTIONAL LITERACY PROJECT

Started in 1967-68 as an inter-ministerial project for farmers training in functional literacy, it aimed at popularisation of high-yielding varieties of seeds through the process of adult education. The programme was confined to 144 districts of the country where nearly 8,640 classes were organised for about 2.6 lakh adults.

NON-FORMAL EDUCATION

In the beginning of the Fifth plan, a programme of non-formal education for people falling in 15-25 years age group was launched. Although the scope, content and objectives of the non-formal project was clearly spelt out, its understanding in the field was very limited and the programmes actually organised were indistinguishable from the conventional literacy programmes.

POLYVALENT ADULT EDUCATION CENTRES

Workers social education institutes and polyvalent adult education centres were reviewed by a group in 1977, which recommended adoption of polyvalent adult education centres in the adult education programme for workers in urban areas. In pursuance of this decision, Shramik Vidyapeeths were set up in the states.

EDUCATION COMMISSION

Constitution of Education Commission (1964-66) was a significant event in the history of education in India. Among several measures, it recommended that high priority be accorded to ending illiteracy. It urged that adult education be promoted both through "selective" as well as through "mass approach" and stressed the active involvement of teachers and students and the wider use of the media for the literacy programme.

The Education Commission also stated that in the world of science and technology, the main objective should be to relate it to life, needs and aspirations of the people so as to make it an instrument of socio-economic and political change.

FUNCTIONAL LITERACY FOR ADULT WOMEN (FLAW)

The scheme of Functional Literacy for Adult Women (FLAW) was started in 1975-76 in the experimental ICDS project areas. It was gradually expanded along with the expansion of ICDS upto the year 1981-82. However, the Planning Commission decided to stop the expansion of FLAW scheme in ICDS project areas mainly due to resource constraint.

The aim of the FLAW scheme was to enable illiterate adult women to acquire functional skills along with literacy, to promote better awareness of health, hygiene, child care practices and to bring about attitudinal changes. The target age group was 15-45, with greater attention to those in the 15-35 age group.

NATIONAL ADULT EDUCATION PROGRAMME (NAEP)

The first nation-wide attempt at eradication of illiteracy was made through the National Adult Education Programme launched on October 2, 1978. It was a massive programme aimed at educating 100 million non-literate adults in the age group of 15-35 years within a time frame of five years.

The objectives of the National Adult Education Programme are not merely to impart literacy in the conventional sense, but also to provide learners with functional awareness, conceived as three integral component skills of reading, writing and arithmetic. Functionality implies the ability to utilize and apply the skills efficiently by the neo-literate in their day-today functioning. The social awareness component is aimed at knowing, understanding and taking action on issues which affect the individual, community and society.

RURAL FUNCTIONAL LITERACY PROJECT (RFLP)

This was a major centrally sponsored scheme started in 1978 in rural areas. The erstwhile 144 farmers functional literacy projects and 60 non-formal education projects were merged into it. Furthermore, new projects were added bringing the total number of projects throughout the country in 1987 to 513, each having upto a maximum number of 300 adult education centres and each centre having 25-30 learners.

STATE ADULT EDUCATION PROGRAMME (SAEP)

The states also similarly took up centre based projects under the state plan funds on the lines of RFLPs.

ADULT EDUCATION THROUGH VOLUNTARY AGENCIES

To ensure greater participation of voluntary agencies, the central scheme of assistance to voluntary agencies was revived in April, 1982. Under this scheme, registered societies were sanctioned centre-based projects for functional literacy and post literacy, and were allowed to run projects in a compact area.

REVIEW NATIONAL ADULT EDUCATION PROGRAMME

Intended to be a mass programme, the National Adult Education Programme (NAEP), however, remained a traditional centre-based programme based on honorarium, hierarchical and government controlled. As against the target of 100 million, a total of 44.22 million learners were enrolled in adult education centres upto March, 1988. On the basis of sample evaluation studies, it has been estimated that only about 45 per cent of the enrolled learners attained literacy. Thus, the level of achievement of this programme in relation to the target set for it was only about 20 per cent. The centre-based programme was reviewed and evaluated by several institutes of social science research and later, the Government of India also appointed a review committee headed by Prof. D.S. Kothari to assess the strengths and weaknesses of the programme. The strengths and weaknesses of the NAEP as revealed through various evaluation studies are summarised below:

Strengths

- Women's motivation and participation had been high.
- Coverage of weaker sections of the society (SCs and STs) was higher than the target.
- The project approach to management adopted for adult education programme is feasible.
- The quality of teaching-learning materials prepared by the National Resource Centre and the State Resource Centres was found to be positive.
- The programme worked well where special recruitment procedures were adopted.

Weaknesses

- Quality of training of the functionaries was poor.
- The learning environment in the adult education centres was poor.

- Mass media did not provide appreciable support.
- Voluntary agencies did not receive willing co-operation from State Government. The existing procedures for their involvement were discouraging.
- There was no linkage between basic literacy, post-literacy, follow-up and continuing education, resulting in the relapse of large number of neo-literates into illiteracy.
- Achievement levels of literacy were below the desired level.
- Training of adult education functionaries at all levels lacked participatory and communicative skills.
- Political and administrative support of the State Government and the Panchayati Raj Institutions was not forthcoming.

NATIONAL LITERACY MISSION

The National Literacy Mission was launched on May 5th, 1988 to impart a sense of urgency, seriousness and emphasis to adult education with fixed goals, a clear time frame and a defined target group, in a mission mode of management. National Literacy Mission has been conceptualised and built on an objective assessment of the strengths and weaknesses of the earlier programmes emanating from the evaluation studies. Creation of mission for literacy represents a national political commitment on the need to harness social forces and channelise the energies of people towards meeting the ultimate objective of effecting a qualitative change in their own lives. The mission seeks to impart functional literacy to non-literate persons in 15-35 age group.

In qualitative terms, functional literacy implies:

- Self-reliance in 3 R's.
- Participation in the development process.

- Skill improvement to achieve economic status and general well-being.
- Imbibing values of national integration, conservation of environment, women's equality and observance of small family norms etc.

The NLM seeks to achieve these objectives through the following means:

- By creating an environment conducive to teaching-learning process, provision of good and relevant teaching-learning materials and facilitating teaching-learning by good training, media and communication;
- By improving the pace of learning and injecting confidence among the learners about their potential to learn and making the process a pleasurable experience.
- By integrating basic literacy with post-literacy and continuing education; and
- By developing the quality of human resource at all levels such as instructor, supervisor, project officer, etc., through orientation and training.

Literacy Curriculum

NLM has defined the desired level of competencies in the 3 R's as follows:

Reading

- Reading aloud, with normal accent, and at a speed of 30 words a minute, a simple passage on a topic of interest to the learner.
- Silent reading at 35 words a minute, of small paragraphs in simple language.
- Reading with understanding the road signs, posters, simple instructions and newspapers/ broadsheets designed for neo-literates.

- Ability to follow simple written passages relating to one's working and living environment.

Writing

- Copying, with understanding, at a speed of 7 words a minute.
- Taking dictation at 5 words a minute.
- Writing with proper spacing and alignment.
- Writing independently, short letters and applications, and filling in forms of day-to-day use to the learner.

Numeracy

- Reading and writing numerals 1-100.
- Doing simple calculations (without fraction) involving addition and subtraction upto 3 digits and multiplication and division by 2 digits.
- Working knowledge of metric units, weights, measures, currency, distance, area and unit of time.
- Broad idea of proportion and interest (not involving fractions) and their use in practical situations.

IMPROVED PACE AND CONTENT OF LEARNING (IPCL)

All adults are neither uniformly endowed nor have the capacity to learn at a uniform pace. Their ingenuity for learning, receptivity and retentivity are varied. Research has also established that adult learners are motivated to learn better if:

- The duration of learning is neither too long nor too short.
- The content of the materials is in conformity with the learners' needs.
- The learners are able to perceive the progress of learning from stage to stage.

Keeping this basic pedagogical findings in view, a new method of learning has been formulated and adopted by the National Literacy Mission. It is known as Improved Pace and Content for Learning (IPCL), its characteristics are indicated below:

- There are three sets of primers, each primer being an improvement on the other in terms of progression.
- Each primer is an integrated one in the sense that it combines work book, exercise book, tools of evaluation of learning outcome, certification, etc.
- The primers are prepared through workshops involving creative thinkers, writers, linguists and artists, pre-tested and their suitability affirmed before actual application.
- There are exercises at the end of every lesson over three tests in each primer.
- The entire exercise is based on the principle of self-evaluation and confidence (rather than competition) oriented evaluation. The tests are intended to be simple, non-threatening and participatory.
- Every learner is free to attain the desired level according to his/her leisure and convenience. It is, however, expected that a learner should be able to complete all the three primers within 200 hours of instruction spread over 6-8 months.

MASS CAMPAIGN APPROACH

Between 1988 and 1990, the National Literacy Mission tried to consolidate the earlier centre based programme to make its implementation more effective. There was no change in the strategy and the centre-based programmes continued. The changes which were brought about in the reorganisation mainly consisted of streamlining various activities and correcting managerial deficiencies. Detailed guidelines for project formulation and implementation were laid down and administrative and supervisory control was vested with the state governments.

One notable exception to the centre-based approach and an experiment with the campaign mode was first seen in Kottayam city in Kerala. Here the district collector, by mobilising 200 volunteers from the local university and forging links with 2000 non-literates in the 6-60 age group, succeeded in making them fully literate within three months.

But, the real breakthrough came with an experiment in mass literacy campaign initiated in 1989 and successfully completed in 1990 in the Ernakulam district of Kerala. The campaign for total literacy here saw fusion between the district administration headed by its collector, volunteer groups, social activists and others and was spearheaded by the Kerala Shastra Sahitya Parishad (KSSP). Ernakulam achieved this objective on 4th February, 1990 and along with it, the unique distinction of being the first distinct in the country to become 'fully' literate.

The principal shift in strategy adopted in the Ernakulam experiment was a change to a well co-ordinated, comprehensive and identifiable initiative. It also marked a change by altering the social context in order to generate demand for the programme and further to sustain it. It established the feasibility of a mass-based, community-based, campaign approach with the objective of generating environment and demand for literacy followed by literacy instruction. The subsequent adoption of the campaign has taken firm root and has given rise to the Total Literacy Campaign (TLC) approach. Drawing inspiration from the success achieved in Ernakulam, entire Kerala, Goa, UT of Pondicherry and several districts in Karnataka, Andhra Pradesh and West Bengal have taken up the challenge for achieving total literacy in a given time frame. These TLCs had a snowballing effect and campaigns were launched in quick succession all over the country.

TOTAL LITERACY CAMPAIGN

The Total Literacy Campaign model is now accepted as a dominant strategy of eradication of adult illiteracy by almost all States/Union Territories. This strategy has been reviewed and endorsed by the National Development Council and by the conference of Chief Ministers of states convened by the Prime Minister on February 15, 1994. TLCs have certain features which make them unique and distinguish them from other government programmes:

- These campaigns are area specific, time bound, volunteer based, cost-effective and outcome oriented. The thrust in TLCs is on attainment of pre-determined norms of literacy and numeracy. The learner is the focal point in the entire process and measurement of learning outcome is continuous, informal, participative and non-threatening.
- The campaigns are implemented through district level literacy committees which are registered under the Societies Registration Act as independent and autonomous bodies to provide a unified umbrella under which a number of individuals and organisations work together. The leadership to this body is provided by the District Collector/Chief Secretary and Zilla Parishad (district council). All sections of the society are given due representation in the planning and implementation of the programme. On the basis of the Ernakulam experience, an organisational structure for a district TLC has been evolved. The structure rests on 3 pillars of (1) Participatory people's committees; (2) Full-time functionaries and area co-ordinators; and (3) A support system provided by government officials, in itself, this may not seem significant, but it exemplifies an interactive and a communicative process of management and implementation.
- The campaign approach to total literacy is characterised by large scale mobilisation through a multifaced communication strategy. The success of the campaign rests substantially on the effectiveness with which all sections of society are mobilised.

- No targets are fixed from the top. The targets emanate from the grassroot level on the basis of a detailed door-to-door survey conducted by the volunteers. This survey is not only a head counting exercise, but also a tool of planning, mobilisation and environment building.
- The campaign is delivered through volunteers without any expectation of reward or incentive.
- The management information system in a campaign is based on the twin principles of participation and correction. It has, to be accountable, credible and instead of being enrolment oriented, it has to be outcome oriented.
- To enable every learner to achieve measurable levels of literacy, the new pedagogy known as "Improved Pace and Content of Learning" (IPCL) has been translated into a set of multi-graded and integrated teaching-learning materials and training. The learner is placed at the focal point in the entire process which, through compact duration and continuous ongoing evaluation, helps to heighten the learner's motivation and improve the pace of learning.
- Training of all functionaries involved in the campaign is crucial to the success of the campaign. Training has to be primer-specific participative, communicative and a tool of continuous correction, upgradation and human resource development.
- Though the TLC is meant to impart functional literacy, it also disseminates a 'basket' of other socially relevant messages such as enrolment and retention of children in schools, immunisation, propagation of small family norm, promotion of maternity and childcare, women's equality and empowerment, peace and communal harmony etc.

So far, TLC projects have been launched in 448 districts out of the total of over 550 districts in the country. Of the districts taking up TLCs, 234 districts have completed the first phase of imparting basic literacy skills and are now implementing post literacy and continuing education programmes. Besides the district-wise literacy campaign projects, the NLM has, since its inception, been promoting illiteracy eradication efforts through literacy projects taken up on a smaller scale under its other schemes, such as, the scheme of assistance to voluntary agencies, rural functional literacy programme, etc.

Literacy projects sanctioned so far under all the schemes of NLM are estimated to cover 148 million non-literates in the age group 9-35. Of them, nearly 119 million have been enrolled and over 72.55 million have already been declared literate. The cumulative number of literacy volunteers mobilised since the launching of literacy campaigns exceeds 10 million. The literacy campaigns thus represent the largest ever civil and military mobilisation in the history of the country.

POST LITERACY CAMPAIGNS

Total literacy campaigns have shown that there is considerable enthusiasm to learn as opposed to the traditional view that learners are disinterested or inhibited has proved to be a myth. TLCs have resulted in a positive change in attitude, to upgrade their skills and adopt it for individual development, and eventually for social action.

Yet, experience all over the world has shown a wide variation in the levels of literacy achieved by individual learners. While a large number achieve literacy levels laid down by the NLM; a significant number do not and many remain non-starters. Even those who do achieve prescribed literacy levels, acquire only 'fragile' literacy. Without a meaningful post-literacy programme, many of them relapse into illiteracy. The more backward the region, more deprived the learning environment, and greater the possibility of relapse. Studies have also shown that one of the major causes of relapse is the time-gap between conclusion of the basic literacy phase and the beginning of post-literacy phase.

Recognising the need for post-literacy programmes, the National Literacy Mission has laid considerable emphasis on timely planning, preparation and launching of a two year post-literacy programme for neo-literates soon after the conclusion of the total literacy campaign. Since post-literacy programmes also rely considerably on the campaign mode, these are commonly described as Post-Literacy Campaign (PLCs). PLCs include about 50 hours of guided learning through a volunteer-teacher to enable the learner to reach a self-reliant level of learning. The subsequent phase of the PLC consists of self-directed continuing education through library service, newspapers, group discussions and other activities such as skill development and vocational training. The Post-Literacy Campaigns addresses itself to the following major objectives:

Remediation

- Those not covered by TLC to be made literate.
- Those below minimum level of learning to be enabled to achieve it.

Continuation

- Stabilisation, reinforcement and upgradation of learning.

Application

- To living and working conditions.

Communitisation

- Group action for participation in development process.

Skill Training

- Life communication and vocational skills.

Post-literacy programmes conceived by NLM are only not remedial measures to ensure retention and stabilisation of listening skills but also an effort of life long education.

NLM has permitted and encouraged high flexibility and innovation in designing and implementation of PLCs. Each

PLC project has to take into account the competence levels reached by the learners in the basic literacy phases cognitive ability, felt needs and other area and socio-cultural specific dimensions.

The approach most commonly followed, comprises of providing post-literacy primer/graded textual material to the learners in the first phase of post literacy for a guided study with the help of volunteer-instructors. This phase specifically aims at remediation, retention and consolidation of literacy skills. In the second phase, the learners are provided with a variety of supplementary reading material and library services to help them continue learning through self-directed processes. In practice, the post-literacy strategies actually being implemented are generally a combination of different approaches, borrowing successful elements from a variety of experiences.

CONTINUING EDUCATION PROGRAMME

Currently, post-literacy programmes are being implemented in 193 districts in the country. The remaining districts are expected to take up post-literacy programmes within the next one or two years. The crucial question is how literacy and the learning environment will be sustained once the district taking up TLCs conclude the two year follow-up programme of PLCs. The enthusiasm and confidence generated among learners in the districts which have successfully completed both the TLC/PLC phases clearly points towards the need to sustain the educational process and to provide learning opportunities on a continuing basis.

National Literacy Mission is fully conscious of this need and was designed a scheme of continuing education for neo-literates. This scheme has been approved by the Government of India and has come into force from January 1, 1996. This scheme replaces the existing post-literacy and continuing education scheme, which was launched in 1988 to meet the post-literacy and continuing needs of the neo-literates emerging from centre-based adult education programmes. The main objective of the new scheme is to institutionalize continuing education for neo-literates and provide considerable flexibility in designing and implementation of a diverse kind of continuing education programmes suited to the felt needs of the neo-literates.

Continuing education is also an indispensable aspect of the strategy of human resource development and of the goal of creation of a learning society. Many of the third world countries and the developing countries are now recognising that socio-economic planning alone is not enough and that the human resource development is a key enabling factor in development. All these countries are aware that education and human resource development will play a key role in the 21st century. What is more significant is the realisation that expansion of formal education alone, which is only a small component of life long learning, cannot lead to human resource development. Formal education as an instrument of human resource development is not really effective in remedying the structural inequalities in the society. Continuing education, which provides a second chance to those missing formal education and is responsive to learner's needs, directly addresses itself at structural inequalities. Only continuing education can bring about full development of human resources. Since continuing education is the opportunity to engage in life long learning, it is now emerging as the main component of the broader view of education.

Objectives of the Continuing Education Programme

The main objectives of the scheme and the activities aimed under it include the following:

- Provision of facilities for retention of literacy skills and continuing education to enable the learners to continue their learning beyond basic literacy.
- Creating scope for application of functional literacy for improvement of living conditions and quality of life.
- Dissemination of information on development programmes and widening and improving participation of traditionally deprived sections of the society.

- Creation of awareness about national concerns such as national integration, conservation and improvement of the environment, women's equality, observance of small family norms etc., and sharing of common problems of the community.
- Improvement of economic conditions and general well-being as well as improvement of productivity by organising short duration training programmes, orientation courses for providing vocational skills and by taking up linkage activities for establishing direct linkage between continuing education and development activities.
- Provision of facilities for library and reading rooms for creating an environment conducive for literacy efforts and a learning society.
- Organisation of cultural and recreational activities with effective community participation.

Beneficiaries

The beneficiaries of continuing education programmes would include the following:

The neo-literates who completes the functional literacy/ post-literacy courses under TLC/PLC or other programmes;

(a) School drop-outs;

(b) Pass-outs of primary schools;

(c) Pass-outs of non-formal education programme; and

(d) All other members of the community interested in availing opportunities for life-long learning.

Establishment of Continuing Education Centres (CECs)

Since continuing education is, by definition, provision of opportunities for life-long learning, setting up local community based CECs becomes indispensable for effective implementation of any continuing education programme. The following guidelines are, therefore, being provided for establishment and organisation of CECs:

- Establishment of CECs should be planned with an area-specific and community based approach.
- One CEC may be established for each village to serve around 500 neo-literates in a population of about 1500 to 2000. However, in thickly populated areas, the population covered may be more than 2000. In sparsely populated areas such as hilly tracts, tribal and desert areas, the population covered could be less than 1500.
- A CEC may be housed in a school building, panchayat ghar or any other public building.
- 8 to 10 CECs would form a cluster, with one of them being designated as a 'Nodal CEC'.
- The incharge (prerak) of the Nodal CEC would be a full-time worker and those of other CECs would have to be volunteers working on part-time basis.
- The Nodal CEC besides undertaking the functions of CECs would facilitate networking with other CECs in the cluster for:

  (a) Providing avenues and facilitates for CE programmes through structured and unstructured modes.

  (b) Conduct for all information, programmes of CE, vocational training etc.

  (c) Supply of books on regular basis.

  (d) Regular monitoring and evaluation.

  (e) Co-ordination with other development departments for convergence of their services at the CECs.

  (f) Establishing, liaison with village education committees, gram panchayats, mahila mandals, voluntary organisations, etc. For active involvement of the community in the CE programmes.

(g) Nodal point for resource mobilsation and decentralised supply of material, equipments, books, etc.

- Supervision of all CECs in a block would be the responsibility of the block co-ordinator, who would liaison with incharge (prerak) Nodal CEC.
- The ZSS will have overall responsibility for ensuring efficient functioning of the CECs in the district. It should establish networking arrangements to foster linkages with development programmes of other departments, secure involvement of NGOs and ensure that peoples' participatory structures at all levels are established and effectively involved in management of CECs and implementation of the continuing education programmes.

FUNCTIONS OF CONTINUING EDUCATION CENTRES

The principal objective of establishment of CECs is to secure as a window or a focal service point where diverse kinds of CE programmes and activities are taken up to provide opportunities for life-long learning to all sections of the population. The functions of CEC would include:

An Evening Class

For upgradation of literacy and numeracy skills to be organised for 3-4 hours once a week. The learners would have the option to come for an hour or so at the time of their convenience on the day.

A Library Reading Room

Books would be purchased from the non-recurring and recurring provisions; copies of old journals, wall papers and newspapers, appropriate for adult learners, informative and entertaining journals, developmental literature etc.

A Charcha Mandal (Discussion Group)

For discussing on common problems, this forum could be utilised for quality of life improvement and individual interest programmes.

Training Programmes

Simple and short duration programmes relating to subjects like health and family welfare, new developments in agricultural and animal husbandry, conservation of energy, improved chulha, etc. CECs may also help the local youth to benefit from various vocational training programmes. Income generation programmes, up-gradation of vocational skills to enable them to take up income generating activities.

Sports and Adventurous Activities

The stress being on indigenous sports, walking excursions, cycling trips in groups, etc. If savings are available, visit to development projects could also be arranged.

Recreational and Cultural Activities

Particularly traditional and folk forms of art, rural theatre, puppetry, etc.

An Information Window

For securing information on various developmental programmes. Information and material suitable for neo-literates may be procured from the concerned development agencies.

A Communication Centre

Where community radio, audio cassette player-cum-recorder may be provided. (In the model CEC only)

CONTINUING EDUCATION PROGRAMMES

Zilla Saksharata Samithis will be encouraged to develop and take up implementation of target-specific programmes catering to the specific needs and interests of neo-literates. Continuing educational programmes would largely be functional in the sense that these would focus on development of functional knowledge with the aim of making learning relevant to living and working. The scheme has the following four components:

Equivalency Programmes (EPs)

Equivalency programmes provide an opportunity to adults and out-of-school children who have completed primary education and who are willing to continue their education beyond elementary literacy for acquisition of competencies informal. system. Equivalency programmes are, therefore, designed as alternative education programmes equivalent to existing formal, general or vocational education.

Income Generating Programmes (IGPs)

Participants acquire or upgrade vocational skills enabling them to take up income generating activities. The major components of IGps may include:

(a) A bridge course to upgrade literacy and to promote social and technological awareness.

(b) Skill development programmes covering commonly required basic skills, trade skills, on-site training and relative trade theory to provide scientific understanding, and

(c) Entrepreneurial skills including book-keeping, marketing and money saving etc.

Quality of Life Improvement Programmes (QLIPs)

QLIPs are especially significant type of educational programmes designed to enhance the well-being of all citizens. Essential knowledge, attitudes, values and skills to enable them to improve quality of life as individuals and as members of the community.

There can be several important elements or aspects of quality of life like biological, social, economic, humanistic and positive societal change with respect to these indicators through education.

Individual Interest Promotion Programmes (IIPs)

These continuing education programmes aim to provide opportunity for individuals to participate in and learn about their social, cultural, spiritual, health, physical and artistic interests.

CONCLUSION

National Literacy Mission is conscious of this need and was designed a scheme of continuing education for neo-literates. The main objective of the new scheme is to institutionalize continuing education for neo-literates and provide considerable flexibility in designing and implementation of a diverse kind of continuing education programmes suited to the felt needs of the neo-literates. To be specific objectives of the continuing education centre as envisaged by the scheme are: provision of facilities for retention, continuing education and application of functional literacy, dissemination of information, creation of awareness about national concerns, improvement of economic condition, improved productivity, recreation and healthy living etc. In order to achieve the above, the continuing education centres has to perform specific functions viz., organisation of evening classes, maintaining library and a reading room, conducting training programmes of short duration, organising charcha mandal, conducting sports and games, recreational and cultural activities and act as an information window and communication centre. The efficiency of the continuing education centre lies on the effective performance of various roles by the prerak. In view of this, the present study is formulated to study the functioning of continuing education centres in Nellore District of Andhra Pradesh. The study is specially devoted to assess the preraks performance and problems, community opinion on prerak performance and the performance and problems of neo-literates.

2

REVIEW OF LITERATURE

Research studies, focussing attention on different aspects of the functioning of post-literacy and continuing education may throw light on the ways and means of organising continuing education centres effectively. The preraks are the actual doers and one of the key elements for the successful organisation of the programmes. In view of this, the present study is formulated to evaluative the functioning of continuing education centres in Nellore District. Further, it is also intended to study the performance and problems of preraks and neo-literates. Empirical investigations with well structured tools and methodologies are scanty if any and they lacked comprehensiveness in covering all possible samples like preraks, community, neo-literates, etc. A few research studies have been identified and presented with a view to get better insight into the research problem to be attempted.

The studies are presented under the following heads:

- Review of studies relating to the performance of the preraks/volunteers.
- Review of studies relating to the problems of the preraks/volunteers.
- Review of evaluation studies relating to the Total Literacy Campaigns.
- Review of studies relating to the problems of the neo-literates.

REVIEW OF STUDIES RELATING TO PRERAKS PERFORMANCE

Muthuchamy (1992) studied the role performance of the preraks working in Rural Functional Literacy projects of

Tamil Nadu and found that there is a discrepancy between the ideal performance and actual performance of preraks in their role as organizes of literacy/post literacy activities (56.25%), generator of awareness (62.60%), organizer of cultural and recreational programmes (56%), mobilizes of resources (60.64%), recording educational activities (35.20%), professional devotion (61.20%), guidance (65.86%), supervisory functions (38.88%). Further, the study also indicated that women preraks, preraks with more than 30 years of age, other than S.C. preraks, better qualified, more experienced are found to be the best role performers.

Nair, Omanna and Rehim (1992) evaluated the programmes and activities of JSN organised by Nehru Yuva Kendra in Kerala. The findings reveal that equal number of men and women are involved as preraks and majority of them fall in the age group of 19-20 years and their annual income ranging from Rs.1,000 to 2,000. Nearly half of the preraks belong to backward communities.

The study also indicates that majority of the preraks had adequate experience as instructors and master trainers in Total Literacy Campaign and majority of the preraks are affiliated to some cultural or sports organisation, their interest in social work motivated them to join as preraks.

With regard to physical facilities, one third of the JSNs have improvised teaching aids, half of them have separate reading room, none of them are having their own building. The source for the books and other material are found to be Nehru Yuva Kendras for majority of the JSNs and all of them are receiving newspapers. The dropouts, inadequate training and funds are the major problems of the JSNs.

Vasumathi (1992) studied the functioning of the Scheme of Jana Shikshana Nilayam in Kannur District of Kerala and found that majority of the Jana Shikshana Nilayams were catering to about 100 to 500 beneficiaries. She also found that majority of the users of Jana Shikashana Nilayam are neo-literates, mostly women. All the JSNs have adequate functionaries and a separate building with and reading room electricity facility.

With regard to the background of the preraks, it was found that majority of the preraks had up to 5 years of experience as instructors and affiliated to some cultural and sports clubs. Further findings are that all the programme officers were men, majority of them have not undergone any training in literacy and not satisfied with regard to the facilities provided to them. Further they have not received adequate co-operation from their higher-ups in organising training programmes, supply of teaching learning materials, mobilising resources etc. All the JSNs have organised various cultural and co-curricular activities such as Literacy Jathas, street dramas, meetings, awareness campaigns, study tours and family meetings.

The study also identified the problems and difficulties of Preraks such as lack of adequate funds, lack of co-operation from the Governmental departments, lack of interest among the neo-literates, inadequate neo-literate literature, inadequate physical facilities, lack of play ground, lack of adequate public support, etc.

Adilakshmi (1993) looked into the working conditions of the JSNs and found that the preraks are confined to the post-literacy activities alone. None of the JSNs are provided with audio-visual aids. One of the findings of the study is that there is no difference in the working according to the age and experience of the preraks.

Reddeppa (1993) identified the determinants of preraks effectiveness which special reference to Rayalaseema Region of Andhra Pradesh. The aim of the study is to measure the effectiveness of preraks, relationship between prerak, effectiveness and their characteristics and also to find out the differences between prerak effectiveness scores representing different groups. The study revealed that the preraks selected for organisation of JSNs were new from unprivileged sections, belonged to agricultural background from lower income groups with less education, less experience, married and belonged to younger age group. Association between prerak characteristics and effectiveness revealed from all sources of ratings that they are significant. Further, sex and effectiveness are significantly associated from learners point of view. The means effectiveness are significantly associated from learners point of view. The mean effectiveness scores reveal that women preraks were found to be more effective. Preraks belonging to forward caste were found to be more effective followed by backward caste group preraks with agriculture background than other groups. Preraks with more income were found to be more effective than lower income groups. Preraks with more education were found to be more effective. Preraks in the higher age groups were found to be more effective than younger age group preraks.

Operations Research Group (DAE, 1994) has evaluated the functioning of the scheme of Jana Sikshana Nilayams and highlighted its strengths and deficiencies. The findings are presented in four subheads viz., Overall Impact, Participation of the Target in JSN Activities, Catering Capacity of JSNs and Infrastructure and Resource Support.

Overall Impact

The continuing education programme, on the whole, has a positive impact on the rural population. The provision of JSN facilities has succeeded in enhancing the demand for education, particularly continuing education, which is apparent from high participation levels. The need for grass-roots level institutions catering to continuing education in being acutely felt in post-TLC districts.

Participation in JSN Activities

(a) Library—The library is found to be the most popular activity of the JSN and is used by people from all age groups. There is a strong demand for a more versatile library facility and for adoption of a decentralised process of selection of reading materials. There were more books available to cater to formally educated than the neo-literates.

(b) Sports, recreational and cultural activities—sports was observed to be the second most popular activity of the JSN. Availability of sports equipments and musical instruments had served

the purpose of making the JSN more attractive to the rural people. However, in most JSNs condition of sports materials was found to be bad.

(c) Literacy classes—Holding of evening classes is perceived to be an important function of the preraks by the community and a majority of the preraks did organise such classes. Largest share of evening class attends were semi-literates from Adult Education Programmes.

(d) Discussion groups—The general level of awareness among the learners groups regarding charcha mandals organised through JSNs was observed 'to be very low'. Charcha mandals catered mostly to exclusively male groups and there is not much participation by women largely because of the conservation social norms and the dual responsibilities which they have to perform at home and in the field.

(e) Training programmes—Organising training programmes has been found to be most neglected activity of the JSNs less than 20 per cent of the preraks reported to have organised any such activity. Also, JSNs were hardly used by other Government departments to impart training or knowledge regarding various schemes or any other developmental issues.

Catering Capacity of JSns

The norm of having one JSN per 5,000 population was found to be too optimistic. In practice, each JSN caters to less than 250 people. For hilly states like Mizoram, the concept of having one JSN to cover 4-5 villages becomes redundant because of conditions of terrain and refused accessibility which clearly indicates that separate set of norms will have to be evolved for allocating JSNs in different regions.

Infrastructural/Resource Support

(a) No budget has been provided for training of preraks and in most of the states, the preraks

deployed to run the JSN's have not received any training at all. Selection of the preraks in many of the states has not been made in accordance with the prescribed criteria. In places where village education committees were associated in the selection process, the preraks chosen were found to be more acceptable to the community.

(b) Shortage of manpower and infrastructure available to the District Adult Education Officers (DAEOs) have adversely effected the supervision and monitoring of the programme. No specific budgetary provisions have been made in the programme to cover expenses on supervision and monitoring. After the withdrawal if RELP, no formal posts of Project Officers or Assistant Project Officers exist to provide an organisational structure for the management of the JSNs. This lack of manpower and absence of adequate interaction between the DAEOs and the preraks have adversely affected the programme performance.

(c) Delays in payment of honorarium to preraks have effectively reduced the commitment level leading even to closure of JSNs, insufficient amount of honorarium is also perceived to be one of the major reasons for non-performance of preraks. Crucial out of pocket expenses of the preraks like organising training programmes, travelling and postage costs are not reimbursed through the programme, which has further hampered the performance of the JSNs.

(d) In most states, the expectation of donation of a space by the community to run the JSN have not been realised. The current JSN programmes does not have a budget provision for reimbursing the amount paid for rented accommodation. Quite often, preraks have been forced to run the JSNs from their own residences which has drastically hindered community participation.

Soundarapandian (1994) conducted a study on the socio-economic status of volunteer instructors and dropout learners of total literacy campaign in Kamarajar District of Tamil Nadu. Two villages in a union project and two wards in municipality project were selected for the study. Majority of the volunteers were in 15-35 years age group (83.53 per cent) women, unmarried, belonged to Backward Classes, SCs and STs and had qualifications above the school level.

The State Resource Centre of Karnataka (1995) conducted an observational study to identity the role of JSN in continuing education. The findings of the study are as follows:

- Majority of the libraries of JSNs are kept open between 8 A.M. to 10 A.M. and 4 P.M. to 6 P.M. and a few of them are kept open through out the day;
- Educators visit JSNs to read newspapers only. However, school going children/school dropouts are the regular users of JSNs;
- Story books and thrillers are found to be popular;
- Inadequate availability of professional, vocational and employment related books;
- Majority of the preraks lacked motivation, insight and vision for running JSN and failed to meet the expectations of public in terms of needs, skills and training of the local youth;
- Although majority of the preraks are well qualified, no evidence of success of JSNs in terms of furthering literacy and continuing education;
- No evidence and support for the claims of conducting cultural, sports and other literacy activities;
- A large quantity of quality reading materials is kept ideal. Preraks are unable to bring awareness in the public. Both preraks and public are indifferent to the spirit and mission of JSNs;

- Facilities provided to the preraks to carry out their duties effectively namely bicycle, sewing machines, radio two-in-one are missing from JSN or they are misused by the prerak and the public. Sports material and musical instruments required replacement and repair;
- Only 5 per cent of the JSNs are found to be functioning effectively in one aspect or the other;
- Only 37 JSNs had its own buildings;
- The post-literacy centres, the Grama Shikshana Samithis have become almost ineffective/ dysfunctional;
- Preraks of the JSNs are under paid and delay and disorganisation in the payment;
- Payment of contingent grants to all the functioning JSN involved bureaucratic procedures;
- A great deal of administrative and inter-departmental procedures involved in providing electricity to JSNs;
- The functioning of JSNs in the state with no buildings of their own area are struggling for their survival because of the interference of donor institutions or other extraneous factors like theft, lack of place, remoteness etc.; and
- The JSNs have been ignored willfully with regard to their role in TLCs and education for all. JSNs have neither place nor responsibility in the network of any of their movement. As a result they are neither obligated to nor accountable to literacy movements.

Dinesh Babu (1996) has studied Instructor's involvement in Continuing Education Programmes at Kulathupuzhal Panchayat of Kerala. The sample for the study is 40 instructors randomly selected. The findings of the study are as follows:

- Majority of the instructors involved in continuing education programmes are females.
- Majority of instructors belong to the age group of 20-30 years.
- 70 per cent of the instructors are Hindus.
- Most of the instructors had passed SSLC examination.
- Majority of the instructors had no technical education and a few are diploma holders.
- Occupational profile of the instructors reveal frequent unemployment among them.
- Most of the instructors earn below Rs. 200/- per month.
- Active participation from Mahila Samajams is found in the CEP.
- Majority of the instructors reported that the organisation of training, method of instruction, content of training and training materials are satisfactory.
- Majority of the literacy centres functioned at the residences of the learners.
- A large number of literacy centres functioned six days per week.
- More than 50 per cent of the instructors spent two hours per day in their job.
- Majority of the centres had need based facilities.
- Nearly 55 per cent of the instructors had no support from the academic council.
- Major problems faced by instructors for conducting the literacy centres are of financial nature.

Adinarayana Reddy (1999) studied the functioning of Jana Sikshana Nilayams in Rayalaseema Region of Andhra Pradesh. The major findings of the study are as follows:

- Majority of JSNs are located in panchayat offices and at preraks residence. Most of the JSNs functioned in the night for about one hour and are electrified. Almost all the JSNs have poor housing facilities and does not have adequate furniture and book keeping facilities.
- The profile of the working preraks reveal that preraks belonging to women, forward caste, labour, more income, more experienced, more educated, married, elders were more positive and effective.
- Association between personal characteristics and effectiveness of the prerak reveal that caste of the preraks is found to be closely associated with their effectiveness.
- The reading material supplied to the JSN and the reading interest of the neo-literate JSNs are found to be closely associated.
- The study also reveals that prerak effectiveness also affects the JSNs performance. In other words, JSN's will be more effective if they are manned by efficient preraks.
- It is evident from the findings that there is a close association between the attitude of the prerak and efficiency of the functioning of the JSNs.
- The JSNs manned by the preraks with moderate problems were found to be more effective than the preraks with more problems.
- The JSNs with more community support were found to be more effective than the JSNs with less community support.

Raja Rao (1999) conducted a Study of Jana Shikshana Nilayam in Visakhapatnam District of Andhra Pradesh. In this district 56 JSN's are located, of them 24 JSNs are selected for the study, 16 of them are from Anakapalli and of them 8 prerak areas were selected. The sample was drawn from 5 categories of respondents namely participants, preraks.

Functionaries (Adult Education Dept.), local elders and local officials. The statistical calculations like percentages, mean and chi-square tests for individual items and rank order methods are carried out. The findings of the study are as follows:

- With regard to the training programmes of the preraks, 85.42 per cent of the preraks and all functionaries are positive while 80 per cent of the functionaries expressed negative view.
- The preraks (56.25%); participants (63.54%); local elders; functionaries (93.33%) and local officials (77.08%) expressed low and medium level of response about official co-operation.
- Regarding the importance given in appointing women as preraks, the preraks (66.66%) expressed good. and very good level of response. and functionaries (86.66%) expressed satisfactory and good level of response.
- Prerak's functions are diversified and wide, the preraks (91.66%); and the local officials (74.44%) expressed medium and high level of response. The participants (88.06%) and the local elders (77%) expressed no and low level of response.
- The participants (42.18%) expressed that the accommodation is not adequate. 26.04 per cent expressed that there are no play ground facilities. 20.31 per cent expressed that there are no lighting facilities and (19.79%), 2 cases expressed that furniture is not adequate. No proper accommodation for women.

Syam and Bhaskaracharyulu (1999) evaluated Continuing education centres in Srikakulam District of Andhra Pradesh. The findings of the study are as follows:

- Majority of the preraks are men 137 (78.73%), half of them belongs to the 26-35 years age group and majority of them (63.7) are B.Cs.

- 98 per cent of the preraks worked satisfactorily.
- 95 per cent of the preraks were trained, 98 per cent of the preraks were conducted review meeting regularly. 70 per cent of the preraks sent their reports in-time to the concerned authorities.
- Preraks faced the problems like lack of teaching materials, co-operation in the village, co-operation by the V.E.C.C., co-operation from the officials (MLO, APO, PO) delaying release of matching grant, lack of proper accommodations, no supply of newspapers and journals.
- The opinion of the MLOs was positive. They received adequate training, provided good environment, conferences and public and mandal level meetings were held. Training programme for preraks were organised, regular supply of teaching and learning materials, inviting the experts etc.

Bharathi (2000) conducted a study on the influence of training, attitude and community support on the performance of preraks of the continuing education centres in Chittoor District of Andhra Pradesh. The sample of the study consisted of 160 preraks and statistical techniques like 't' test, 'F' test and multiple regression analysis (step-wise) were used while analysing the data. It was found that sex and level of education significantly influenced the performance of preraks whereas age, caste and experience had no significant influence on the performance of preraks. The trend of the mean training scores revealed that men preraks had better training than the women preraks, preraks representing higher age group 30 years and above obtained a better training score in relation to the lower age group (less than 30 years), the forward caste group preraks secured a better training score than the preraks representing the Backward Castes, Scheduled Castes and Scheduled Tribes. The better qualified preraks (Degree and above) secured a better mean (Intermediate and SSC) and those possessing better experience obtained a better training score in relation to those who were short of experience.

Further, duration of training significantly influenced the performance of preraks.

Viswanadha Gupta and Janardhana Reddy (2000) studied the functioning of continuing education centres in Chittoor District of Andhra Pradesh in terms of the profile of the preraks, location of the centres, supply of materials, attendance of learners, co-operation from CE Committee and problems of the preraks. The findings of the study shows that majority of the preraks are male, middle aged, graduates, BCs and with two years experience. Furthermore half of the working preraks are not trained but happy with the honorarium they received. More than three fourths of the CECs are located in public buildings and with sports material, two daily newspapers and 200 to 800 titles of post literacy materials. Response of the target shows that the co-operation from CE members is inadequate. With regard to the problems of the preraks, lack of proper building, irregular supply of electricity, heavy work load, meager and delay of payment of honorarium, etc., were found to be the major problems.

Reddeppa (2001) conducted a study on Jana Chaitanya Kendras (JCKs) in Chittoor District with special reference to monitor effectiveness. The results of the study revealed that monitors belonging to men, forward caste, social workers possessing better education, income and experience performed better in organising the post-literacy and continuing education activities. The mean performance scores of the sample revealed that monitors representing the married group had obtained better performance scores and the performance of monitors was positively associated with the availability and utility of physical facilities in the centres.

Vasantha Kumari and Sudha Rani (2002) conducted a study on the constraints of continuing education programme. Data was collected from 100 members of continuing education centres and 25 preraks in different villages of Nellore District. It was noted that 25.00 per cent of the preraks were qualified upto tenth class, 35.00 per cent had Intermediate qualification and the remaining 40.00 per cent were graduates. Only 35.00 per cent of the preraks were satisfied with their job. Majority of the preraks were men. 53.00 per cent of the preraks organised different educational programmes regularly.

Krishna Murthy (2003) conducted a study on the performance of preraks in Anantapur District with the objectives of identifying the roles performed by the prerak and the level of performance of the roles as perceived by preraks. The results of the study based upon the checking of the item by at least half of the sample are as follows:

Roles Performed by Preraks under the Category 'Very Good' (70% and above)

- Creation of awareness among the beneficiaries about national concerts.
- Motivating the dropout learners to attend the centres.
- Securing the help of mandal literacy organiser and adult education observers.
- Keeping the books, magazines, newspapers etc., for use by the beneficiaries.
- Procuring leaflets, books, magazines from development departments.
- Participating in prerak's training programme and review meetings.
- Maintaining cordial relations with the neo-literates and members of the village.
- Participating in development programmes like Janmabhumi, Clean and Green etc., along with the beneficiaries of continuing education centre.
- Securing the co-operation of Gram Panchayat, learners association, youth clubs, Mahila Mandals, self-help groups, voluntary organisations etc., in organising the activities of the centre.
- Maintaining the equipment of the centre (almirah, book racks, petromox light, table, charts, chairs, roller board, games materials, cycle, etc.).

- Submitting monthly/quarterly/half-yearly and annual reports to Mandal and District officials.
- Identifying dedicated and committed volunteers for mopping up operation programmes.
- Entering the financial aspects and checking the accounts.

Roles performed by the preraks under the category 'Good' (50-70%)

- Publicising the importance of continuing education programme.
- Recording the activities organised at the centre.
- Creating favourable environment to achieve the objective of educational for all.
- Celebrating important days (World Literacy Day, Independence Day, Gandhi Jayanthi, etc.) at the centre.
- Providing books, magazines, neo-literate literature etc., to neo-literates to read at home during their leisure time.
- Helping the neo-literates to understand and read easily several reading materials.

Roles Performed by the Preraks Under the Category 'Average' (30-50%)

- Organisation of evening classes for learners (neo-literates, semi-literates, illiterates etc.).
- Organisation of cultural activities at continuing education centre.
- Displaying the basic data of the village (population, education, health, development programmes etc.) at the continuing education centre.
- Organisation of recreational activities, sports and games at continuing education centre.

- Securing the help of village education committee in organising the activities.
- Devoting time for self-development to organise the activities of the continuing education centre in the best manner.

Roles Performed by the Preraks Under the Category 'Poor' (0-30%)

- Conducting the activities of Charcha Mandal.
- Organisation of lectures and demonstration programmes with the help of resource persons at continuing education centres.
- Organisation of income generating programmes for the benefit of the beneficiaries.
- Procuring/purchasing charts, pictures etc., for the use at the centre.
- Enabling the neo-literates to get benefitted from development programmes.
- Securing the physical, financial and human resources support (resource persons) for organising different awareness programmes.
- Maintaining managership and accountability for the activities of the centre.
- Undertaking innovative programmes and identifying innovative methods of teaching literacy skills.

Roles Performed by the Preraks Under the Category 'Not at all Performing' (Zero per cent)

- Taking steps to help the neo-literates to appear for 5th class/7th class examinations.
- Organising programmes to promote mental peace, happiness, values, sincerity, patience, etc., among the beneficiaries.

- It was found that gender, age and education influenced the performance of preraks.

REVIEW OF STUDIES RELATING TO PROBLEMS OF THE PRERAKS

Muthuchamy (1992) identified the problems of the preraks in performing the roles prescribed for the preraks and Rural Functional Literacy projects of Tamil Nadu. The identified problems of the preraks in organising Jana Sikshana Nilayams are lack of interest among the people for learning, lack of effective planning, inadequate physical facilities and proper place for JSN, non-availability of graded materials, lack of sufficient training for the preraks, limited knowledge possessed by the preraks, inadequate supply of neo-literate materials, lack of motivation on the part of learners, lack of transport facilities, inadequate audio-visual aids, difficulty in bringing the experts to the villages, inability of the prerak in contacting the specialists, resource personnel, non-availability of local talents; non-existence of mahila mandals and youth clubs, lack of measuring instruments of functionality and awareness among the adults, lack of technical/professional skills, inadequate training of personal and social problems faced by the preraks. In addition to the above, the study also found that women preraks of over 30 years, other than the SCs are better qualified, more experienced are found to be the best role performers.

Kumara Swamy and Padmanabhaiah (1995) identified the problems faced by the monitors at the grassroot level in Chittoor District of Andhra Pradesh. Findings of the study are as follows:

- The monitors have identified the areas of problems viz., physical facilities, administrative matters, learners and community support.
- With regard to gender difference in perceiving the problems men and women monitors of the sample differed significantly on problems like lack of permanent accommodation to JCKs; negligence on the part of government officials and ZSS to solve the problems of monitors and learners; unlimited

number of works to be performed by monitors; lack of involvement of village sarpanches in JCK activities; involvement of political leaders; lack of supervision to JCKs by mandal resource persons and panchayat co-ordinators; lack of interest to mandal education officer to visit JCKs; and lack of time of mandal development officer. Among these problems, lack of permanent accommodation to JCKs; Negligence on the part of government officials; and involvement of political leaders significantly were more common to men and the remaining 5 problems are more severe to women.

Janardhan Rao (1996) studied the problems faced by monitors in Janachaitanya Kendras of Chittoor District and the findings are as follows:

- The association between caste and problems relating to the 'organisation' and co-operation are found to be significant.
- There are no significant differences between the monitors belonging to different groups. They did not differ significantly with each other on the problems of administration of Jana Chaitanya Kendras. However, the monitors belonging to OC, BC and SC/ST differed significantly on this item. The monitors' age and experience is not suitable to discuss about the village problems in charcha mandals. The monitors with different occupations differed significantly on the item lack of suitable sports and games materials at the Jana Chaitanya Kendras. In addition to the above, the monitors with different income background also differed significantly on the item "charcha mandal activities were affected due to the village politics and lack of special care for the backward learners".
- There is significant difference between the monitors belonging to different castes and occupational groups in the problem area

'environment' as a whole. The item wise analysis reveals that monitors belonging to different occupational and experience groups differed significantly on the item lack of audio-visual aids to disseminate the information to the learners in Jana Chaitanya Kendras.

- The aspect wise ability to motivate the neo-literate for continuing education was found to be significantly differed among the monitors belonging to different occupational and educational groups. The monitors belonging to OC, BC and SC/ST groups experience differed significantly on the problem of lack of equal participation on the part of men and women in the activities of Jana Chaitanya Kendras.

Mohanty and Prusty (1996) identified the problems of functioning of JSNs in Orissa and the findings of the study are as follows:

- Majority of the JSNs are situated near to the home of sarpanch or chairman and not suitable to the learners.
- Half of the JSNs lacked basic infrastructure and learners faced trouble in reading at centres in summer and rainy seasons.
- No library and TV or Radio facilities.
- JSNs did not receive adequate teaching material and in time. Even the quality of the supplied material was of low quality.
- Though charcha mandals are working in many JSNs local people have not benefited by them as they did not give due importance to local needs, occupations, professions having practical or income orientation.
- Instruction for women on their daily life are negligible.

- Finances are mismanaged and corruption is rampant.
- Majority of the preraks are regular and highly educated. Though some exceptionally highly educated preraks tried to act democratically their hands were tied by higher authorities. Some also suffered from financial crisis and lack of conscious support from local people to activate JSNs.
- Cultural activities like Ganesh Puja, Saraswathi Puja, Independence day were observed, but neglected the important days like World literacy day, World health day, Environmental day, Netaji Jayanthi etc., which are not know to rural illiterates and neo-literates.

Surya Prakasham G. (2000) made an enquiry into the Problems of Preraks of Continuing Education Centres in Tirupati Revenue Division. 50 preraks for the study were selected randomly in Tirupati Rural Mandal. The findings of the study are as follows:

- Majority of the preraks are in the age group of 21-30 years followed by the age group of 31-40 years.
- Half of the preraks are with intermediate qualification and another 38 per cent are graduates.
- Majority of the preraks belong to backward classes.
- Majority (68%) of CEC's are managed by men preraks, whereas women preraks constitute only 32 per cent.
- Organisational problems are, delay in the payment of honorarium to preraks, inadequate training for preraks, inadequate keeping of records and registers.
- Personal problems of the preraks are low level of education, inadequate understanding about government schemes, etc.

Janardhana Rao, V. (2002) identified the problems of the volunteers in 100-day literacy programme of Chittoor District. The main findings of the study are as follows:

- The intensity of the problems encountered by the volunteers working in 100-day literacy programme is not similar.
- The more prominent problems of the volunteers were found to be non-availability of audio-visual aids, services of development departments, co-operation from programme administration, insufficient duration of the programme, lack of avenues for functional skills, lack of suitable physical facilities at the centre etc.
- Prominent problems of the volunteers constitute lack of suitable facilities, difficulty in solving the personal and social problems, difficulty in generating empowerment among women, political interference, volunteers personal problems, lack of information on women and child welfare.
- The less prominent problems of the volunteers includes lack of upto date information on developmental programmes, unable to distribute learning materials in time, lack of interest among the learners, difficulty in identifying learners progress and reporting to higher authorities, difficulty in identification of proficiency attained by the learners in arithmetic, non-acceptance of volunteers other than participants caste.
- There is a significant association between type of the family of the volunteer and his problems.
- There is a close association between age, education, occupation, experience and number of children of the volunteers and problems in the area of organisation and management. Further, it is also found that there is significant difference between the volunteers belonging to different groups of occupation, experience, marital status, type of

family in their problems in the area of organisation of management.

- The association between personal characteristics and problems of the volunteers in the area of teaching and learning revealed that the association is significant in case of sex, caste, education, marital status, type of family, number of children, radio and urban contact.

Vasantha Kumari et. al. (2002) identified the problems faced by the volunteers in attending the Akshara Sankranti Programme in Nagalapuram Mandal of Chittoor District. Major findings of the study are as follows:

- 49 per cent of the sample felt that there is lack of library facilities.
- 48 per cent of them felt that not even minimum facilities are provided in the centre.
- 46 per cent of the volunteers are of the opinion that there was no co-operation from the officials.

REVIEW OF EVALUATION STUDIES RELATING TO THE TOTAL LITERACY CAMPAIGNS

Saldana (1992) evaluated the literacy campaign in Wardha District and the findings of the study are as follows:

- The learners based on their scoring were divided into four grades i.e., A, B, C, D, 1.76 per cent of the tested sample achieved grade A with 60 per cent and above marks. 15.4 per cent obtained grade B with 45 to 59 per cent marks, 2.7 per cent achieved grade C with 35 to 45 marks and 5.7 per cent achieved grade D scoring less than 35 per cent marks.
- Both males and females generally scored higher marks in numeracy as compared to their respective performance in reading and writing. On the other hand 67.9 per cent of the males and 60 per cent of the females attained grade A in numeracy as

against 28 per cent and 20.2 per cent in reading and writing. The mean score of the total sample in numeracy is 76.17 per cent.

- The overall achievement on the cut-off-point prescribed by EET i.e., scoring of 35 per cent aggregate was 99.4 per cent in the case of males and 93 per cent in the case of females. The achievement of SCs and STs was 98.4 per cent and 95.9 per cent respectively. The mean scores of successful candidates in reading, writing and numeracy are 73.42, 43.39 and 76.66 per cent respectively.
- The achievement of the sample learners according to the NLM norms comes to 47.24 per cent and 52.2 per cent for men and women respectively. On the other hand, 44.1 per cent and 46.0 per cent in the case of SCs and STs respectively.

Anil Bhatt (1993) evaluated the Tumkur District literacy campaign as per NLM norms (40 marks reading, 30 each for writing and arithmetic) and found that 71.55 per cent of the sample is able to attain 50% of marks in each of the 3 R's viz., reading, writing and arithmetic. In addition to the above, over 90% of the adult learners scored minimum marks of 50% in reading and numeracy. However, writing was found to be critical skill and most difficult to acquired. Performance of the children in the age group of 9-14 years was better (79.2%) than that of those in the age group 15-35 (77.5%). The performance of the persons who are working was found better than those who are not working. Further, the study also indicates that the performance of males over females and STs over SCs is found to be better.

Evaluation of literacy campaign in Jalna was conducted by Deshpande (1993) of Indian Institute of Education and the following are the findings:

- 20,109 learners appeared in the test and 17,781 were found qualified according to the NLM norms with an overall result of 88.42 per cent. The pass percentage of the males is 89.20 per cent and the female 88.04 per cent.

- Average scores of both males and females are almost same i.e., 81.17 per cent and 80.65 per cent respectively which proves that female learners in Jalna District are equally competent as that of men.
- The performance of young learners in the age group of 9-14 in the district is as good as or in some cases a little better than that of the adult learners.
- In the comparative performance of total learners in reading, writing and numeracy, the writing ability with 72.23 per cent mean scores is the lowest when compared to numerical ability with 83.96 mean scores and reading ability with 80.2 mean scores.

Indra Deva and Rajasekhar (1993) evaluated TLC in Bilaspur of Madhya Pradesh State, the results of the study indicate that:

- 74 per cent of the learners attained the norms.
- The SC learners fared well in two sub-projects i.e., Matsuri and Pangarlu with 91 per cent and 87 per cent success. In the third project Seepat they attained only 54 per cent.
- Among tribal sub-projects, Belghana, Kota, Pali and Haridibazar achieved success rate of 85 per cent and 83 and 67 per cent respectively.
- Average score secured by the successful learners in reading, writing and numeracy is 81, 66 and 87 per cent.

Krishnamurthy BH and others (1993) evaluated the T.L.C. campaign of Chittoor District. The major findings of the study are as follows:

- The T.L.C. in Chittoor has resulted in raising the literacy level.
- The literacy attainment of the target population in the age group of 9-35 years is 64.3 per cent as per the NLM norms.
- Majority of the participants of the T.L.C. belong to SC, ST and BC.
- Majority of the selected sample consisted of women and agricultural labour.
- Only 12.7 per cent of the selected sample had some schooling earlier.
- 78 per cent of the sample gained A and K grades. Caste wise analysis shows that over 80 per cent of SCs. 79 per cent of OCs, 78 per cent of STs and 74 per cent of BCs obtained grades between A and C. Female learners fared better than the male learners. 64.3 per cent reached the prescribed level of literacy. The study suggests that the reading material was of poor quality and requires association of experts of different disciplines.

Prem Chand (1993) evaluated the TLC of Dungarpur in Rajasthan and the findings are as follows:

- Out of the 3891 learners, 3574 (91.9%) achieved level 'A', scoring more than 70 per cent of marks, 272 (7.0%) scoring 50 to 70 per cent marks and 45 (1.1%) achieved level 'C' scoring less than 50 per cent marks. Out of the achievers of grade A, 1155 out of 1220 are males and 2,419 out of 2,671 are females.
- 90.5 per cent, 87.6 per cent and 76.3 per cent of the learners achieved grade 'A' in numeracy, reading and writing respectively.
- 55.17 per cent in the age group 6-9, 90.39 per cent in the age group, 9-14 and 92.29 per cent in the age group 15-40 achieved grade 'A'.

Rokadia (1993) evaluated the TLC of Ajmir (Rajasthan). The following are the findings of the evaluation. Out of the total of 6,694 learners evaluated, 4,536 or 85.01 per cent achieved level 'A' (with 80 per cent and above marks) 695 or 10.85 per cent achieved level 'B' (with 70 to 79 per cent marks) and 26.3 or 4.11 per cent achieved level 'C' (with 60-69 per cent marks). Thus, the total outcome of the external evaluation is 89.22 per cent.

Sardhar Patel Institute of Economic and Social Research (1993) evaluated the Kheda District literacy campaign. The study revealed that 86.2 per cent of the learners are successful. As far as awareness is concerned 97.7 per cent learners are aware of personal cleanliness, 45.6 per cent are aware of immunisation programme, 58.11 per cent are family welfare programme, 56.55 per cent are aware of sanitation in and around the houses. In addition, 87.16 per cent are aware of development programmes. 78 per cent are aware of social aspects like dowry system, social evils, minimum age for education, removal of un-touchability and family planning etc.

Tata Institute of Social Sciences (1993) evaluated TLC in Lathur. The evaluation reveals the following:

About 82 per cent of the evaluated learners scored above 50 per cent marks in the literacy test as per the EET norms and 49.7 per cent as per the national literacy norms. As per the NLM norms, 58.4 per cent of the males, 45.2 per cent of females, 51.6 per cent of the learners in rural areas and 38.95 per cent of the learners in the urban areas achieved success in the test. The success of SCs and STs is 46 per cent in reading, writing and arithmetic. It was found that the mean performance is good in numeracy than in reading and writing.

Tata Institute of Social Sciences evaluated the TLCs in Nanded (Maharastra), 1993. The findings of this study are:

The learning outcome on the basis of literacy test is 82.7 per cent, 58.8 as per EET norms and 90.8 per cent of males evaluated are declared qualified according to the EET norms. On the other hand, 70.7 per cent qualified according to the NLM norms, (61.8 per cent of the learners scored more than

70 per cent marks, 20.9 per cent 50 to 70 per cent marks). The achievement rate of SCs, STs and minority communities comes to 58.8 per cent. The achievement in different literacy abilities of reading, writing and numeracy is 81.2 per cent, 75.5 per cent respectively. 82.7 per cent scored 50 per cent or more marks. Overall achievement of literacy is 41.90 per cent. In terms of the number of months of learning, those who had fewer than six months of learning performed poorly while who had more than six months of instruction performed satisfactorily.

Centre for media studies (1994) conducted a pilot study for evaluating the literacy campaign of Panipat, Haryana State. The findings revealed that 1/3 of the sample achieved 70 per cent of marks. The female learners performed better than the males. Achievement of the adults was better than that of children in the age group of 9-14 years. The target groups performance in writing is 20.9 per cent and the achievement in other two components i.e., reading and numeracy is double than the writing.

Kishore Attaver (1994) evaluated the Shimoga district literacy campaign and found half of the learners tested achieved NLM norms in literacy. The comparative performance of the men and women revealed that men scored more than women. Age-wise achievement show that the children in the age group of 9-14 years scored better (52.38%) than the 15-35 age group (50.30%). The STs fared better (75.83%) than, the SCs (55.55). With regard to the achievement in various literacy abilities 80.41 per cent of learners in reading, 79.37 per cent in numeracy and 42.70 per cent in writing ability attained 50 per cent or more marks.

Misra (1994) of Vikram University evaluated the TLC in Ratlam (Madhya Pradesh) and found that

- 86.46 per cent of the sample neo-literates reached the NLM norms of proficiency.
- Distribution of neo-literates according to their total score shows that 45 per cent of the neo-literates obtained the score of above 80 followed by the score

of 70-79 by 31.27 per cent and only 13 per cent obtained less than the score of 60.

- Letter writing was the weakest point, achievement in reading, writing and numeracy and oral questions were calculated as 92.03, 75.77, 70.27 and 79.06 per cent respectively.
- Achievement in rural areas ranged from 69.53 to 91.19 per cent while in urban areas it ranged from 69.53 per cent to 98.26 per cent.

Mushtaqu Ahmad (1994) evaluated the TLC in Almora and the findings of the study are as follows: the learners outcome of this district was 40.3 per cent on the NLM norms. Some villages deemed best by the ZSS, were also separately tested. Their outcome came to be only 38.1 per cent which is less than that of the whole district. Among the blocks, the performance of Kapal proved to be the best with 49.3 per cent.

Sardar Patel Institute of Economic and Social Research (1994) evaluated the literacy campaign of Dang district of Gujarath. The findings of the study shows that 62 per cent of the sample learners secured 50 per cent of marks in aggregate and only 23.93 per cent secured 70 per cent marks in aggregate. The out come of male learners is better than that of the females and 66 per cent Scheduled Tribes candidates have scored more that 50 per cent. On the other hand only around 33 per cent belonging to SCs. Bakshi panch and others have secured 50 per cent and more. Occupation wise 80 per cent labourers have secured more than 50 per cent of the marks.

Sardar Patel Institute of Economic and Social Research (1994) evaluated the literacy campaign of Sundar Nagar District. The study shows that more than 86 per cent of the neo-literates scored 50 per cent marks and while 22 per cent secured 70 per cent and above marks in literacy test. The achievement in reading, writing and numeracy is found to be 83 per cent, 62 per cent and 88 per cent respectively.

NIRD evaluated the literacy programme in Chittoor District (1994). The study reveals the following learning outcomes:

- The cut-off points for declaring the learners successful in the test was taken as 50 per cent a deviation from the NLM norms of scoring 70 per cent in aggregate and 50 per cent marks in each of the reading, writing and arithmetic abilities. Thus, 81.6 per cent of the sample learners succeeded in literacy test. With regards to the division wise analysis, 95.38 per cent success rate was recorded in Chittoor Division followed by 77.8 per cent in Madanapalli and 71.2 per cent in Tirupati Division.
- The average score for the sample is 67.27 (63.82 in case of females and 71.85 in case of males). The mean scores of SCs, STs and BCs are found to be 64.87, 61.55, 66.86 and 72.10 respectively.
- It was found that female agricultural labourers secured less marks than their counterparts.
- Marital status of the learners has no relationship with the learning process.

Sidday Gowda (1996) evaluated the Akshravani programme of Chitra Durga district of Karnataka. The findings of the study are as follows:

- The target set for the literacy achievement was 413932 but only 131226 were evaluated. Out of this, only 32.97 per cent attained NLM norms.
- 71.06 per cent of neo-literates have scored more than 50 per cent of marks in numeracy. However, the performance in writing skills is only 46.06 per cent of neo-literates achieved 50 per cent of marks. On the other hand, reading occupies second position with 66.84 per cent scoring more than 50 per cent of marks.

- There is not much difference between men and women in their achievement. As a whole, 33 per cent of men have scored more than 70 per cent of total marks with a minimum of 50 per cent marks in each skills where as 32.95 per cent of women achieved the same.
- 50.73 per cent of Christians followed by Muslims with 47.7 and Hindus with 36.96 per cent have scored more then 70 per cent of marks.
- Occupation wise, agriculturists (40.82) stood first followed by house wives and (38.33%) coolies (36.6%). All these occupational groups have scored more than 70 per cent of marks.
- Performance of the neo-literates in the age group of 15-25 years, 25-35 years shows that 38.04 and 37.98 respectively have scored more than 70 per cent of marks. The result demonstrates that age is neither a criteria nor a bar for learning.
- Income wise analysis shows that 37.9 per cent of the neo-literates in the lower income group less than Rs. 5000 per annum and 42.11 per cent in the higher income group of more than Rs. 15000 per annum have scored more than 70 per cent marks.
- Agriculture festivals (Harvest festival) season and personal reasons are found to be major reasons for dis-continuation of learning.
- Major reasons for dropout are work load, personal problems, no support at home, learning difficulty, no personal interest.

Institute for Development Research and Alternatives (2001) evaluated the Akshara Sankranthi Programme in Khammam District. The findings of the study are as follows:

- 48.79 per cent of the learners attained the NLM norm.

- Attainment of learners in the 3 components of literacy shows that all the 4 divisions of the sample have attained more than 80 per cent in reading. In the case of writing Palvancha stood first with 74.81 per cent followed by Khammam (72.94%) and Kothagudem (71.93%). Bhadrachalam with 67.21 per cent is lagging behind compared to other divisions. In the case of Arithmetic, all the divisions, except Bhadrachalam (79.81%) have crossed 80 per cent.
- Sample belonging to less than 20 years of age group have stood first with 56.15 per cent followed by 21-40 age group (47.43%) and 42.86 per cent above 40 age group.
- OCs and BCs have attained more than 50 per cent. However, in the case of SC and ST, the attainment is 46.90 per cent and 45.36 per cent respectively.
- Learners engaged in labour has attained 78.70 per cent literacy followed by agriculture and other occupations.

REVIEW OF STUDIES RELATING TO THE PROBLEMS OF THE NEO-LITERATES

Prabhakar Reddy (2000) has identified the root causes of low strength in continuing education centres of Tirupati Revenue Division of Chittoor District. The important causes are: lack of time, shyness to attend the centre, fear of the ridicule by the people, no immediate economic benefit, busy with agricultural work, feeling of age not suitable, lack of encouragement from local leaders, appointing non-local people as preraks, unaware of continuing education centres and its duties, lack of interest to continue their education.

Prem Chand (2000) reviewed literacy situations in South India and identified the problems in implementing the Continuing Education Programme. Major problems to be confronted in the implementation of the Continuing Education Programmes include motivating the learners, functionaries, retention of literacy and making use of literacy in their day-to-day life by the target groups, development of functional literacy and skill development. He suggested that voluntary organisations, universities/educational institutions and resource centres.

Vasantha Kumari and Sudha Rani (2000) identified the problems faced by the neo-literates in attending the continuing education centres in Chittoor District of Andhra Pradesh. Centres categorised into seven according to the nature and type of problems like due to lack of basic facilities, preraks problems, curriculum problems, materials and methods, personal and social problems of learners, health problems, family and children problems and problems with regard to work. The major findings of the study are as follows:

- Neo-literates in the age group 25-35 years faced more problems than those in younger age group of 15-25 years.
- Men faced more problems than women to attend the CECs.
- Learners who are engaged in agriculture faced more problems than the others.
- The problems of neo-literates are sometimes influenced by age, sex and occupations.

Harisingh Chowhan (2001) identified the problems of post-literacy campaign and suggested a few solutions for effective implementation of Post-Literacy Campaigns. He has identified the causes for relapsing into illiteracy, dropouts, admitting the semi-literates and illiterates students in post literacy programme, need for co-ordination among workers and lack of constant supervision, monitoring and evaluation.

Jagannada Rao, D. (2002) identified the problems faced by neo-literates to attend continuing education centres in Tirupati rural mandal of Chittoor District. The major problems faced by the neo-literates in attending the CECs were lack of infrastructural facilities, preraks inefficiency of teaching, personal, family, social, economic and health problems, lack of time, heavy work, insufficient reading materials for the neo-literates.

CONCLUSION

From the above review, it is clear that not many studies were conducted on the functioning of the continuing education centres. The available studies were of peripheral and were not able to throw much light on the activities undertaken inside and outside the continuing education centres. The knowledge in the functioning of the continuing education centres in terms of various activities undertaken inside and outside the continuing education centre and in the community will be more helpful in formulating suitable strategies for providing better services and to rectify the defects if any, in the implementation of the scheme.

If the continuing education centres are not able to perform the functions for which they are created, then the entire effort i.e., making illiterates literates will become a wasteful one. Hence, knowledge of the activities that were undertaken inside the continuing education centre and in the community will go a long way in formulating suitable strategies in the effective implementation of the scheme of continuing education centre. As the review of literature has not disclosed much in this direction, the present study is formulated to investigate the functioning of the Scheme of Continuing education centres in Nellore District of Andhra Pradesh.

3

STATEMENT OF THE PROBLEM

This chapter describes the problem, scope and need of the study, functions of the study, objectives, hypothesis, variables incorporated, limitations of the study and definition of certain terms.

STATEMENT OF THE PROBLEM

An evaluative study on the Functioning of Continuing Education Centres in Nellore District, (A.P.).

SCOPE OF THE STUDY

The study enquires into the performance of the continuing education centres with special reference to preraks and neo-literates in discharging their functions as prescribed in Nellore district of Andhra Pradesh. Hence, the aim of the study is to identify the problems encountered by the preraks and neo-literates in their role performance in the continuing education centres. The performance of the preraks is measured in terms of the retention of literacy by the participants of continuing education centres and self-rating of the preraks. Preraks performance is also measured in terms of community opinion. The study also covers the association between socio-economic and demographic characteristics and performance and problems of preraks and neo-literates. The impact of the socio-economic and demographic characteristics of the preraks and neo-literates on their performance and problems are also studied. The study also aims to assess the community opinion on the performance of preraks.

NEED OF THE STUDY

The Government of India launched the National Literacy Mission (1988) to empower the vast masses of the illiterates through literacy, social awareness and functional information not only to accelerate the socio-economic development but also to upgrade them as human resources. In order to realise this, the National Literacy Mission adopted the strategies of Total Literacy Campaign at district level to cover the large number of illiterates by adopting the strategies of area based, time bound, cost effective, outcome oriented and volunteerism. Nellore district of Andhra Pradesh is one of the districts implementing Total Literacy Campaign in the name of Akshara Deepam Programme. The programme now has entered into the third phase viz., continuing education phase after the completion of literacy and post-literacy stages. The external evaluation of Andhra University, Visakhapatnam, the district has revealed that it has achieved 70 per cent of literacy. However, again resurvey was made to identify the illiterates in the age group of 9-35 years. The survey revealed that illiterates came from the groups of new entrants, school dropouts, non-enrollers and dropouts of earlier literacy programme. The survey identified 4 lakhs of illiterates in the district.

The success of any development programme largely depends on the participation of the functionaries, in this case, the preraks and target groups in its implementation from initiation to conclusion. Continuing education centres are no exception, the preraks have to perform multi-dimensional functions and will have to be in constant interaction with a number of clientele viz., illiterates, literates, neo-literates, youth, educated, job holders, development agencies, etc. In this process, they have to make use of various groups of people as resource persons, mobilizers or even as participants of the programme. In the process of elicitation of the participation and support from above groups, the preraks have to face innumerable problems. Further, the performance of preraks also depends not only on the nature of the problems they face but also on the nature of the training they have received and the past experience they have. Further, the performance of the preraks is also closely associated with the achievement of the objectives of the programme.

In the case of the continuing education centres, the ultimate aim is to retain the literacy and help the neo-literates to use it in their day-to-day life for their betterment. Hence, understanding the problems of the preraks and their capacity and competency to motivate the illiterates to join the centres and the neo-literates to retain their literacy will be useful to the programme planners and administrators not only to equip the functionaries to tackle the anticipatory problems in the field effectively but also to help them to know the anticipatory results of their efforts. Keeping in view of the above, the present study is formulated to study the functioning of continuing education centres in Nellore district. The specific functions of the continuing education centres are as follows:

FUNCTIONS OF CONTINUING EDUCATION CENTRES

(a) **An Evening Class:** For upgradation of literacy and numeracy skills to be organised for 3-4 hours once in a week. The learners would have the option to come for an hour at their convenience.

(b) **A Library and Reading Room:** A repository of learning materials and place which encourages people to read.

(c) **A Charcha Mandal:** For discussing common problems, this forum could be utilised for quality of life improvement programmes of individual interest.

(d) **Training Programmes:** For short duration training programmes to upgrade the skills.

(e) **Sports and Adventurous Activities:** The stress being on indigenous sports, walking excursions, cycling trips in groups, etc.

(f) **Recreational and Cultural Activities:** Particularly traditional and folk forms of art and theatre, puppetry, etc.

(g) **Information Window:** For securing information on various development programmes.

(h) **A Communication Centre:** Where community radio, audio cassettes, player-cum-recorder may be provided.

OBJECTIVES OF THE STUDY

The specific objectives of the study are as follows:

Principle Objective

- To study the performance of the continuing education centres with special reference to preraks and neo-literates.

Subsidiary Objectives

- To identify the problems of the continuing education centres with special reference to preraks and neo-literates.
- To study the relationship amongst performance, problems and socio-economic and demographic characteristics of the preraks.
- To study the relationship amongst performance, problems and socio-economic and demographic characteristics of the neo-literates.
- To assess the community opinion on the performance of preraks in organising the continuing education centres.

HYPOTHESES

Keeping in view the above objectives, following hypotheses are formulated for testing.

- The level of performance of the preraks working in continuing education centres is not similar.
- There is no significant association between the socio-economic and demographic characteristics and performance of the preraks working in continuing education centres.
- There is no significant relationship between the socio-economic and demographic characteristics and performance of the preraks working in continuing education centres.

- The intensity of the problems encountered by the preraks, working in continuing education centres is not similar.
- There is no significant difference between the prerak personal problems and programme related problems.
- There is no significant association between the socio-economic and demographic characteristics and the personal problems encountered by the preraks in organising the continuing education centres.
- There is no significant relationship between the socio-economic and demographic characteristics and the personal problems encountered by the preraks in organising the continuing education centres.
- There is no significant association between the socio-economic and demographic characteristics and the programme related problems encountered by the preraks in organising the continuing education centres.
- There is no significant relationship between the socio-economic and demographic characteristics and the programme related problems encountered by the preraks in organising the continuing education centres.
- There is no significant association between socio-economic and demographic characteristics and the problems encountered by the preraks in organising the continuing education centres.
- There is no significant relationship between socio-economic and demographic characteristics and the problems encountered by the preraks in organising the continuing education centres.
- The level of the performance of the neo-literates attending the continuing education centres is not similar.

- There is no significant association between the socio-economic and demographic characteristics and performance of the neo-literates.
- There is no significant influence of the socio-economic and demographic characteristics on the performance of the neo-literates.
- Preraks performance does not significantly influence the performance of neo-literates.
- The intensity of the problems encountered by the neo-literates in attending continuing education centres is not similar.
- There is no significant difference between the neo-literates personal problems and programme related problems.
- There is no significant association between the socio-economic and demographic characteristics and personal problems encountered by the neo-literates in attending the continuing education centres.
- There is no significant relationship between the socio-economic and demographic characteristics and the personal problems encountered by the neo-literates in attending the continuing education centres.
- There is no significant association between the socio-economic and demographic characteristics and the programme related problems encountered by the neo-literates in attending the continuing education centres.
- There is no significant relationship between the socio-economic and demographic characteristics and the programme related problems encountered by the neo-literates.
- There is no significant association between socio-economic and demographic characteristics and

problems encountered by the neo-literates in attending the continuing education centres.

- There is no significant relationship between the socio-economic and demographic characteristics and problems encountered by the neo-literates in attending the continuing education centres.
- There is no significant difference between positive and negative opinions of the performance of preraks.
- There is no significant difference between the preraks performance and neo-literates performance.
- There is no significant difference between the preraks'problems and neo-literates problems.
- There is no significant difference between the preraks performance and community representatives opinion.

VARIABLES INCLUDED IN THE STUDY

As mentioned in the preceding pages, the aim of the study is to study the performance and problems of the preraks and neo-literates. The problem both in the centre and in the community depends not only on their personal characteristics but also on their performance in terms of literacy achievement of the neo-literates. The prerak would be considered efficient despite the problems of he/she succeeds in imparting literacy and its functional aspects to the neo-literates. Further, the performance of the prerak also depends on his day-to-day activities in organising the continuing education centre. The community representatives opinion also depends on the level of performance of the preraks. In order to effectively implement the continuing education programme it is necessary to study the preraks performance and their problems, opinion of the community and neo-literates performance and problems. In view of the above, the following variables are used:

(i) **Dependent Variable:** Three variables viz., performance of the preraks and neo-literates and problems of the preraks and the neo-literates and community representatives on the performance of preraks are considered.

(ii) **Independent Variable:** The socio-economic and demographic characteristics of the preraks and neo-literates i.e., sex, marital status, age, caste, education, occupation, experience, income, type of family and number of children are chosen as independent variables of the study.

LIMITATIONS OF THE STUDY

- The study is limited to the continuing education centres in Nellore district.
- The study is based on a small sample of preraks and neo-literates.
- The continuing education centres performance was measured by taking preraks/neo-literates performance and opinion of the community representatives.

DEFINITION OF CERTAIN TERMS

Prerak : A motivator and an organiser of the activities of continuing education centre.

Monitor : A person who has been organising post-literacy centre after literacy campaign in Nellore District.

Corpus Fund : It is the fund collected for the organisation of the activities of continuing education centre after the cessation of assistance from the government after five years. The fund has to be collected from the beneficiaries, philanthropists and others. A sum of Rs. 10,000/- is expected to be collected from the public and a matching grant of Rs.10,000/- will be deposited by the government and the interest has to be used after five years for meeting the honorarium of the prerak, library books, newspapers and for the organisation of simple and short duration programmes.

Membership Fee : A sum of one rupee has to be contributed by every beneficiary of continuing education per month. It can also be paid as Rs. 6/- for six months at a time or Rs. 10/- per annum at a time. By paying a nominal membership, the beneficiaries will have a right to question the prerak for facilities. About 1500-2000 beneficiaries of CEC, pay membership on regular basis each year, naturally it would be a huge amount which can be added to the corpus fund. Corpus fund and membership fee are specific to Andhra Pradesh and not the policy of National Literacy Mission on continuing education.

Functional Literacy : As specified in the National Literacy Mission document (1988) by Government of India, functional literacy implies achieving self-reliance in literacy and numeracy by learners, becoming aware of the causes of their deprivation and moving towards amelioration of their condition through organisation and participation in the process of development, acquiring skills to improve the economic status and general well-being, imbibing the values of national integration, conservation of the environment, women's equality, observance of small family norm etc.

Equivalency Programme : These are one type of continuing education programmes which provide an opportunity to adults and out of school children who have acquired basic literacy skills or who have completed primary education and who are willing to continue their education beyond elementary literacy for acquisition of competencies equivalent to primary or secondary levels of formal education. Equivalency programmes are, therefore, designed as alternative education programmes equal to existing formal, general or vocational education.

Income Generating Programme : Income generating programmes are those vocational and technical education programmes which help participants to acquire or upgrade vocational skills and enable them to conduct income generating activities. There can be a variety of income generating programmes delivered in a wide variety of contexts taking into account the local needs and interests of learners.

Quality of Life Improvement Programmes : These are especially significant type of educational programme designed to enhance the well being of citizens. These aim to equip learners and community with knowledge, skills, attitude and values to enable them to improve quality of life as individuals and members of the community.

Individual Interest Promotion Programmes : These continuing education programmes aim to provide opportunity to individuals to participate in and learn about their social, cultural, spiritual, health, physical and artistic interests. The focus of individual interest promotion programmes is on personal development by providing opportunities for promotion of specialised individual interests which may lead to improvement in the quality of human resources of the society.

The method adopted in the study in terms of construction of research tool, sample chosen, data collection, statistical techniques employed are presented in the Chapter-4.

4

METHOD OF INVESTIGATION

The continuing education programme is conceived for neo-literates, semi-literates, dropouts of the TLC/PLC, pass outs of primary schools and all other members of the community and new entrants in the age group of 9-35 years. In other words, the preraks who are responsible for instruction should strive hard to fulfill their obligations within a given period of time. As instruction is time bound, the preraks should know their job to be performed and obstacles likely to be faced. Prerak needs to have skill in instruction, creation of favourable environment for nurturing the newly learnt skill of literacy, methods of teaching, understanding the psychology of adults, disseminating the information, etc. Since the prerak is the most important person for the success or failure of continuing education, it is imperative to study the prerak role in running the continuing education centres as well as the achievements of the neo-literates. It is also essential to understand and assess the attitude of the community towards this programme. In order to collect the information relating to the above aspects, tools like preraks performance, preraks problem inventory, achievement test in literacy on neo-literates, neo-literates problem inventory and community opinion, questionnaires on preraks and neo-literates background are required. Review of various tools used in the study clearly demonstrates that the available research tools do not suit the present requirements. Hence, the following tools are developed.

PRERAK'S PERFORMANCE SCALE

As mentioned earlier, prerak is the key person for the organisation and running of continuing education centre.

Hence, the performance of the prerak plays a predominant role in achieving the objectives of the continuing education programme. The performance of the prerak also depends on the educational environment that is created, community background and support, personal abilities of the prerak, his/her exposure to training, the interest, aptitude for the job. Being a grassroot level functionary, he/she has to interact with the neo-literates at the field level and programme administrators at the apex level.

For the purpose of the study, a measure that can rate the performance of the prerak with reference to the roles assigned to him is necessary. The prerak has to perform specific functions viz., organisation of evening classes, maintaining the library with a reading room, conducting training programmes of short duration, organising charcha mandal, conducting sports and games, recreational and cultural activities, acting as a information window and communication centre. In order to identify the performance of the prerak, an enquiry was made to measure the performance of various roles of CEC individually and as a whole. From the review of literature it appears that no systematic attempt has been made by any researcher in the field of adult education to develop and standardize the test that could rate preraks of continuing education. The performance of the preraks needs to be assessed item wise and area wise in a scientific and systematic manner. A rating scale provides more opportunity to clearly rate the performance the preraks in relation to questionnaire and observation. This necessitated the construction of a rating scale for the study to rate the performance of the preraks. In developing the rating scale, the following steps are followed.

PREPARATION OF THE PRELIMINARY FORM

The preraks' performance can be identified by using various methods such as interview, observation, checklist, questionnaire, ratings and other suitable parameters.

First, a list of items supposed to describe the performance of the prerak from different angles were pooled together from different sources like preraks, participants of the programme, administrators of the programme, experts in the field etc. Further, the list thus prepared was supplemented with a list of items drawn from review of literature and the guidelines issued by Government of India prescribing the scheme of continuing education centres and roles to be performed by the preraks. The list thus prepared was submitted to a panel of 5 experts with a request to scrutiny the statements for their appropriateness and for refinement. There are 55 items in the preliminary form of prerak role performance rating scale. Hence, for the purpose of the study, the rating scale method was used.

ADVANTAGES OF THE RATING SCALES

- Rating requires much less time than the ranking method.
- Self explanatory when graphic method is used.
- It can be used with persons of minimum training.
- The range of its application is very wide. It can be used for teaching ratings, personality ratings, testing validity or papers pencil inventories, school appraisal and several others.

TYPES OF RATING SCALE

(i) Numerical scale,

(ii) Graphic scale,

(iii) Descriptive scale

(iv) Cumulative scale and

(v) Standard scale

(i) **Numerical Scale:** In a five-point scale, for example, the "Average" persons scored, the deviants scored +2, +1, -2 or -1, or the scores to eliminate signs can all be positive, I being the lowest, 3 the average, 5 the highest, for example, how was the lesson introduced in the class ?

No.	*Trait*
1.	Very unsatisfactory
2.	Unsatisfactory
3.	Satisfactory
4.	Good
5.	Outstanding

(ii) **Graphic Scale:** A common variant of the scoring method is the graphic rating scale. The several levels, or degrees of the trait are defined and placed at points along a horizontal line. The judge places a mark any where he chooses on this line between the two extremes. Although, a graphic scale theoretically permits scoring a large number of points, such refinement and accuracy are not warranted. This may be expressed as under.

Very High	High	Average	Low	Very Low

(iii) **Descriptive Scale:** The rater puts a check (a) in the blank before the trait which is described in a word or phrase.

Ex.: Do the learner take the initiative?

- Exhibits marked originality,
- Willing to take initiative,
- Quite inventive,
- On the whole un-enterprising and
- Very dependent on others.

(iv) **Cumulative Points Scale:** An individual rates himself. He checks his traits on a list of objectives. He then counts his favourable and unfavourable responses. For each item, there are two responses to be weighed as +1 and 0.

(v) **Standard Scale:** A set of standards is presented to the ratings. Ratings through this scale become easier and more meaningful. For example, man to man ratings of hand writing comparison.

DEVELOPMENT OF THE TOOL

A list of prerak's performance was gathered from different sources like personal interviews with the preraks, village co-ordinators, participants of the programme, based on consultation with the experts in the field and the review of related literature. The items pooled were again rewritten for removing the ambiguous items, items without clarity, repetition and inaccuracies. These items were arranged under different headings. The list thus prepared was presented to a panel of 5 experts and suggestions of the experts are incorporated and finally 45 items are taken for rating.

The preraks performance schedule consists of two sections, section one deals with the data pertaining to the preraks background such as viz., sex, marital status, age, caste, education, occupation, experience, income, type of family and number of children, section two deals with the preraks performance in continuing education centres.

RATING PROCEDURE

For the purpose of present study, numerical rating technique was chosen, keeping in view of its advantages, background of the sample and the opinion of the experts. In rating the items, the popular numerical rating scale consisting of five descriptive cues were chosen. The five descriptive cues viz., strongly agree, agree, undecided, disagree, strongly disagree having the scores 5, 4, 3, 2 and 1 was chosen. The respondents were supposed to agree with any one of the alternative cues and mark the level of performance of the prerak in that particular role under consideration.

Scoring of the Items

S. No.	*Nature of Response*	*Numerical Value assigned*
1.	Strongly Agree	5
2.	Agree	4
3.	Undecided	3
4.	Disagree	2
5.	Strongly Disagree	1

PILOT STUDY

A sample 60 preraks are selected at random from different continuing education centres in Nellore District of Andhra Pradesh. However, care is taken to see that the sample selected represent all the sections of the society. Before administering the scale, the purpose and mode of filling the scale was explained to the preraks.

SELECTION OF ITEMS

To find out the discriminative power and usefulness of the items chosen for prerak performance scale, the 't' values for each of the items in the scale are calculated as per the procedure suggested by Edward (1969). Items that has 't' value equal to and greater than 1.96 were selected for inclusion in the final form and those with 't' values less than 1.96 are discarded.

RELIABILITY OF THE TOOL

There are several methods of estimating the reliability of the scale. Some of the commonly used methods for finding out the reliability of the scale are:

- Test, re-test reliability
- Split-half reliability
- Alternate (or) parallel form reliability
- Kudar-Richardson Estimates

For the purpose of present study Test, re-test reliability of the scale developed was examined. This was done by obtaining the rating for the scale twice with an interval of one month between the first and second administration of the instrument to the same set of (60) preraks. The correlation and coefficient between the rating was 0.92 which is significant at 0.01 level. Therefore, the prerak performance tool used in the study is highly reliable.

VALIDITY OF THE TOOL

Any instrument developed for measuring a particular aspect will be considered appropriate only when its validity is proved. The prerak performance scale developed on the lines described above possess satisfactory validity with reference to the content, items and intrinsic validity. The description of details relating to validity of the scale are as follows:

(i) Content Validity

Content validity means establishment and evaluation of the relevance of the test items individually and as a whole. Every item should be a sampling of that aspect which the test purports to measure. Further, when taken collectively, the items constitute a representative sample of the variable that is measured. The present scale ís developed keeping the above in view. As already described, items for the scale are collected from different sources viz., monitor, preraks, neo-literates and community. Further, they are also supplemented by a review of related literature and also by interviewing selected preraks to make sure that all possible items are included thus it is reasonable to assume that the instrument possess satisfactory content validity.

(ii) Item Validity

Item validity stresses the number of discriminations of the desired sort that the itèm is capable of making. It emphasises the extent to which the item predicts segregation of examines into those with high versus those with low criterion scores. The discriminative power of each of the item of the present scale is established by calculating the 't' values as described above. Thus, the items chosen for the scale are found to be effectively valid.

(iii) Intrinsic Validity

Intrinsic validity indicates the degree to which a test measures what it purports to measure. Thus, it can also be stated as how well the obtained scores measures the tests true score component. Square root of the reliability value of the scale means its intrinsic validity. Thus, the intrinsic validity of the scale is which can be assumed as highly satisfying intrinsic validity score.

BRIEF DESCRIPTION OF THE FINAL FORM OF PRERAK PERFORMANCE

The final form of prerak performance scale developed in the lines described above consisted of two sections. Section-A relates to the background of the preraks and Section-B of the scale consists of job performance items. Each item can be rated on any of the five response categories viz., strongly agree, agree, undecided, disagree and strongly disagree which carries numerical values 5, 4, 3, 2 and 1 respectively. In view of this, the score of the scale will range between 45 and 225 points.

PRERAKS PROBLEM INVENTORY

One of the aims of the study is to identify the problems of the preraks in performing their job. Keeping this in view, the available literature is reviewed and found that not much effort has been made in developing a suitable and comprehensive scale for measuring the problems of the preraks. Hence, an attempt is being made by the investigator to develop a prerak problem inventory on scientific lines not only to identify the problems but also to see the intensity of the problem checked by the preraks.

In developing the problem inventory method mentioned above, the following steps are taken.

(a) Preparation of Preliminary Form

Preraks' problems can be identified and studied by adopting various methods and sources. They can be identified by using various methods such as interview, observation, checklist, questionnaire, ratings and other suitable parameters. The sources of identification of the problems can be personal interview with the preraks, observation of actual proceedings of the continuing education centres, enquiry with the field administrators and others etc.

Each of the above methods and sources has its own merits and demerits. However, for the purpose of the present study, the rating scale method is considered appropriate not only for identifying the problems but also to study their intensity. With regard to the sources, preraks themselves are appropriate source for identification of the problems. Hence, the rating scale method for identifying the problems and their intensity is being used. Further, this method helps in categorising the problems based on their intensity expressed by the preraks.

(b) Development of the Tool

A list of prerak's problems is gathered from different sources like personal interviews with the preraks, village committees, participants of the programme, consultation with the experts in the field and the review of related literature. The items pooled are re-written again for removing the ambiguous items, items without clarity, repetition and inaccuracies. These items are arranged under different sub-headings. The list thus prepared was presented to a panel of 5 experts and suggestions of the experts were carried out. At this stage, there were 45 items in the inventory.

The prerak's problem inventory consists of two sections, section one deals with the data pertaining to the preraks background such as sex, marital status, age, caste, education, occupation, experience, income, type of family and number of children. Section two deals with the prerak problems in the organisation of continuing education centre.

(c) Rating Procedure

As the aim of the study is not only to identify the problems but also to measure the intensity of the problem, appropriate method is a numerical rating scale consisting of five descriptive cues for rating the items by the sample with ease and accuracy. Hence, a five point numerical rating scale consisting of 5 descriptive cues viz., strongly disagree, disagree, undecided, agree, strongly agree with the scores 1, 2, 3, 4 and 5 respectively was constructed. Respondents were supposed to agree with any one of the alternative cues to indicate the intensity of the problems that they were exposed in discharging their roles.

Scoring of the Items

Sl. No.	*Nature of Response*	*Numerical Value assigned*
1.	Strongly Disagree	1
2.	Disagree	2
3.	Undecided	3
4.	Agree	4
5.	Strongly Agree	5

(d) Pilot Study

A sample of 60 preraks representing all social segments of the society were selected at random from different continuing education centres in Nellore District. They were explained the mode of filling the scale so that data gathered is accurate as for a possible.

(e) Selection of Items

Based on the obtained problem scores, the preraks problem inventory response sheets were arranged in descending order. The top and bottom response sheets were chosen to find out the discriminative power and usefulness of the items. The 't' values for each of the items of the two categories of response sheets were calculated and all the items with 't' values of 1.96 and above were retained for the final form and rest of the items with less than the 't' value of 1.96 were discarded as suggested by Edward (1969). Based on the above procedure 10 items were discarded and the final number of inventory consisted of 35 problems.

(f) Reliability of the Tool

For the purpose of the present study, Test, re-test reliability of the scale was adopted. This was done by obtaining the ratings for the scale twice with an interval of one month between the first and the second administration of the scale to the sample. The obtained, correlation coefficient between the two ratings was 0.92 which is significant. Therefore, the prerak problem inventory used in the study is highly reliable.

(g) Validity of the Tool

Any instrument developed for measuring a particular aspect will be considered appropriate only when its validity is proved. Construct validity refers to the extent to which a test reflects constructs presumed to underline the test performance and also the extent to which it is based on theories regarding these constructs. The preraks problem inventory developed on the lines described above possess satisfactory validity with reference to the content, items and intrinsic validity. The description of details of the validity of the inventory is as follows:

(i) **Content Validity:** Content validity indicates how adequate is the content of a test-sampling, the domain about which inferences are to be drawn. Further, when taken collectively, the items should constitute a representative sample of the variable that is measured. The present preraks' problem inventories were developed keeping the above in view i.e., while selecting the items, the functionaries of the programme, researchers and review of literature was consulted. Thus, it can reasonably be assumed that the instrument possess satisfactory content validity.

(ii) **Item Validity:** Item validity stresses the extent to which the item predicts segregation of examiners into those with high versus those with low criterion scores. The discriminative power of each of the item of the present scale was established by calculating their 't' values as described under the heading 'Selection of Items'. Thus, the items chosen for both section of the scale were found to be effectively valid.

(iii) **Intrinsic Validity:** Intrinsic validity, the degree to which a test measures what it purports to measure. This can also be stated as how well the obtained scores measure the tests true score component. Intrinsic validity refers to the square root of its reliability. Thus, the intrinsic validity of the preraks problems inventory was the square root of its reliability $\sqrt{0.92} = 0.96$ which can be assumed that the scores have highly satisfying intrinsic validity. Reliability value of the scale is nothing but its intrinsic validity.

(h) Brief Description of the Prerak Problems Inventory

The final form of the preraks problem inventory developed in the lines described above consisted of 35 items. Each item can be rated on any of the 5 response category namely strongly disagree, disagree, undecided, agree and strongly agree which carried numerical values 1, 2, 3, 4 and 5 respectively. The score on the inventory will range between 35 and 175 points. Since there are 35 items , the least value with the 35 (35 x 1) or 175 i.e., the highest value on the scale (35 x 5).

CONSTRUCTION OF THE ACHIEVEMENT TEST IN LITERACY

For the purpose of the present study, an achievement test in literacy was developed. The measure of achievement in literacy is intended to estimate the level of attainment in reading, writing and arithmetic skills-3R's by the participants of the literacy in continuing programme. The programme participants who have successfully completed the course in continuing education programme should have achieved basic skills-3R's-reading, writing, arithmetic to the extent of fulfilling the norms of literacy stipulated by National Literacy Mission (NLM).

As per the NLM norm, to declare a person as literate he/she has to obtain 50 pr cent of marks in each of the three components and 70 per cent as an aggregate. The above criteria was adopted to arrive at literacy attainment rate among the sample of the neo-literates in continuing education centres.

Keeping in view of the above and based on the National Literacy Mission norms, the investigator has developed 3 sub-tests in literacy viz., reading, writing and arithmetic.

(i) Reading Test

Reading test is intended to identify the level of reading abilities and proficiency achieved by the participants of the programme. Items for the reading test were drawn from the primers used in the Improved Pace and Content of Learning (IPCL) approach. The reading test has 3 units: (a) identification of the picture and slogan, (b) comprehension passage, (c) loud reading and comprehension passage. The above items were decided after taking the opinion of preraks, mandal literacy organizers and experts in the field.

A detailed test method is given below.

(a) Identification of Picture and Slogan

Identification of a picture with a slogan.

(b) Comprehension Passage

A single passage consisting of 18 words and 3 sentences were given on match factory. The examiners were supposed read the passage and answer two questions on the passage.

(c) Loud Reading a Comprehension Passage

A passage consisting 26 words and 6 sentences on self-help groups was given. It was a major item for loud reading of a passage. Neo-literates are categorised in loud reading into three i.e., good, average and poor, marks given are 8, 4 and 2 respectively. Four questions were coined on the passage. The intention of the test is to see the neo-literates capacity to read and understand the given passage.

The preliminary form of the reading test thus finalised is administered to the sample of 180 neo-literates in continuing education centres individually. The data thus obtained are analysed to find out the differences and discrimination level. As suggested by Garott (1979), all the items showing discrimination values of 0.30 and above and difficulty values between 0.40 and 0.60 are considered for inclusion in the final form and rest are ignored.

Scoring Procedure

Sl. No.	*Item*	*Marks for each item*
Unit No. I	Identification of the picture and a slogan (3 + 3)	6
Unit No. II	Comprehension passage (3 + 3)	6
Unit No. III	Loud reading and comprehension passage (8 + 20)	28
	TOTAL	40

The final form of the Reading Test with 3 units and scoring of the test is detailed above.

(ii) Development of Writing Sub-test

A review of the written tests developed by different investigators shows that a comprehensive written test will have 3 sub-tests:

(a) Neo-literate background information

(b) Identifying the picture and writing a sentence.

(c) Writing a memorandum/letter

(a) Neo-literate Background Information

Unit-I is related to the writing of neo-literates name, father's/husband's name, occupation, preraks name and address. Five marks are allocated to the item.

(b) Identifying the Picture and Writing a Sentence

Unit-II, four pictures were given. The neo-literate was expected to identify the picture and write a sentence on each one of them. Two and half marks were allocated to each picture. Thus, the neo-literate can score totally 10 marks in this section.

(c) Writing a Memorandum/Letter

Unit-III related to the writing of a representation by the neo-literate to the District Collector informing about a community problem and requesting him to solve it. 7 marks were allocated to writing address and 8 were allocated to the content, the total marks coming to 15.

A model test paper was submitted to a panel of 5 subject experts for their comments and suggestions were incorporated and the test was administered to continuing education centre neo-literates individually. The data thus obtained were analysed to find out the difficulty and discrimination levels of each of the items included in the test paper. Items showing discrimination value of 0.30 and above and difficulty values between 0.40 and 0.60 were included in the final form.

The final form of writing test was represented by units consisting of neo-literate background information, identification of the picture and writing a sentence and writing a memorandum. The scoring procedure for the writing sub-test in brief is as follows:

Scoring Procedure

Sl.No.	*Item*	*Total Marks*
1.	Neo-literate background information	5
2.	Identifying the picture and writing a sentence	10
3.	Writing a memorandum/letter	15
	TOTAL	30

(iii) Development of Arithmetic Sub-test

Before developing the numeracy test, available arithmetic tests developed in various projects were examined. Arithmetic test usually contained additions, subtractions, multiplications, divisions and problems of any one or combination of the above. In addition, the arithmetic tests also consisted of transfiguring the numbers given in the form of words into numerals. The investigator consulted the experts about the possible items to be incorporated in the test and their suggestions were followed.

The investigator pooled all the possible items arrived at through discussions with filed staff and experts and designed the test with 7 units as described below:

(a) Fill-in the Missing Number

(b-c) *Additions:* Arithmetic operation involving addition of 1, 2, 3 and 4 digit number in 2 and 3 rows of 6 items.

(d) *Subtraction:* Arithmetic operation involving subtraction of 2, 3 and 4 digit numbers of 5 items.

(e) *Depicted time:* Identification of depicted time.

(f) *Multiplication:* Arithmetic operations involving multiplication of 2, 3 and 4 digit numbers with sign and double digit numbers of 4 items.

(g) *Division:* Arithmetic operations involving division of 2, 3 and 4 digit number with single and double digit numbers of 4 items.

Six problems involving simple arithmetic operations namely fill-in the missing number, additions, subtraction, depicted time, multiplication of arithmetic test were submitted to a panel of 5 experts and their suggestions were incorporated.

Preliminary test paper thus prepared was administered to 180 neo-literates of the programme for try out and for finalising the test paper. The data thus obtained were analysed to find out the difficulty and discrimination levels of each of the items in the preliminary test paper. Items showing discrimination values ranging 0.40 and 0.60 were included in the final test paper. The final test paper of arithmetic test consisted of 6 sub-units. The details are as follows:

Scoring Procedure

Sl. No.	*Sub-tests*	*No. of Items*	*Total Marks*
Unit No. I	Fill-in the missing number	6	6
Unit No. II	a. Additions	1	4
	b. Additions	5	5
Unit No. III	Subtraction	5	5
Unit No. IV	Depicted time	2	2
Unit No. V	Multiplications	4	4
Unit No. VI	Division	4	4
	TOTAL		30

RELIABILITY OF THE TEST

The reliability of the achievement test was established by adopting test, re-test reliability of the 3 sub-tests. This was done by administering the entire achievement test to the same set of continuing education centre participants with a gap of one month. The co-relation, co-efficients between reading, writing and arithmetic sub-tests were 0.93, 0.91, 0.89 respectively. The 'r' values of the sub-tests were significant at 0.01 level. In view of this, test is considered having high reliability.

VALIDITY OF THE TEST

The test developed for measuring a particular aspect will be considered appropriate only when its validity is true. The achievement test in 3 R's developed on the lines described above possesses satisfactory validity with reference to the content and intrinsic validity.

NEO-LITERATES PROBLEM INVENTORY

One of the aims of the present study is to identify the problems of the neo-literates. Keeping the need of the present study, the available literature was reviewed to identify a suitable tool for measuring the problems of the neo-literates. The review of the literature revealed that suitable tool required for the present study was not readily available. Hence, the investigator decided to develop a neo-literate problem inventory. In developing the problem inventory method the following steps were taken.

(a) Preparation of Preliminary Form

The neo-literates problems can be identified and studied by adopting various methods and sources. They can be identified by using interview, observation, checklist, questionnaire, ratings and other parameters. The sources of identification of the problems can be personal interview with the neo-literates.

For the purpose of the present study, the rating scale method is appropriate not only for identifying the problems but also to study their intensity with regard to the sources. Further, this method helps in categorising the problems based on their intensity expressed by the neo-literates.

(b) Development of the Tool

In order to develop the inventory a large number of possible problem items were pooled together from different sources like neo-literates, preraks, community, programme administrators, experts in the field etc. The list was also supplemented with a list of items drawn from the review of the literature. The list thus prepared was presented to a panel of 5 experts with a request for scrutiny and suggest additions and deletions. Considering the suggestions of the experts, the list of the problems modified. The list thus prepared consisted of 50 problem items.

The neo-literate problem inventory consists of two sections, section one deals with data pertaining to the neo-literates background such as sex, marital status, age, caste, occupation, income, type of family and number of children and section two deals with the neo-literate problems in attending the continuing education centre.

(c) Rating Procedure

Keeping in view of the background of the sample and opinion of the experts in the field, it was thought that the rating chosen should be as simple as possible to facilitate the sample to indicate the rating with ease and accuracy. The five point numerical scale consists of five descriptive cues viz., strongly disagree, disagree, undecided, agree and strongly agree with scores 1, 2, 3, 4 and 5 respectively. The respondents were supposed to agree to any of the alternative cues to indicate the intensity of the problems that they are facing.

(d) Pilot Study

A sample of 180 neo-literates were selected at random from different continuing education centres of Nellore District for pilot study. Before administering the inventory, care was also taken to see that sample selected represent all the sections of the society.

(e) Selection of Items

Based on the obtained problem scores, the neo-literate problems inventory response sheets were arranged in descending order. The top 27 per cent and bottom 27 per cent response sheets were chosen to find out the discriminative power and usefulness of the items. The 't' values for each of the items of the two categories of response sheets were calculated and all these items with 't' values of 1.96 and above were retained for the final form and rest of the items with less than the 't' value of 1.96 were discarded as suggested by Edward (1969). Based on the above procedure 16 items were discarded and the final form of inventory consisted of 34 problems.

(f) Reliability and Validity of the Tool

The reliability of the tool was established by Test, re-test method. The 'r' value between the two ratings were found to be significant 0.92 at 0.01 level. Further, the validity of the inventory was also established in the form of content validity, item validity and intrinsic validity. In view of the above, the neo-literate problem inventory were found to be highly reliable and valid.

(g) Brief Description of the Neo-literate Problems Inventory

The final form of neo-literate problem inventory developed in the lines described above consisted of 34 items. Each item can be rated on any of the 5 response category namely strongly disagree, disagree, undecided, agree and strongly agree which carried numerical values 1, 2, 3, 4 and 5 respectively. The score on the inventory will range between 34 and 170 points.

COMMUNITY OPINION SCALE

In order to measure the opinion of the community representatives towards various functions of continuing education centres, a measure is required. From the review of the literature, it is clear that there are no suitable tools readily available for measuring the community opinion of the community towards continuing education centres. Hence, the investigator has to develop community opinion scale for the purpose of the present study. Out of the available options for developing community opinion scale, it was decided to develop the community opinion scale.

(a) Preparation of Preliminary Form

As a first step in preparation of the community opinion scale, field functionaries, community, village continuing education committee members were interviewed and generated a list of items depicting the attitude statements. In addition to the above, relevant literature was reviewed, relevant items were pooled and supplemented to the list. The list of descriptive items thus obtained were subjected to scrutiny and relevant statements were added to the list. After this, all the statements together were reviewed and rewritten to avoid ambiguity and overlapping.

Hence, for the purpose of the study, the rating scale method was used through which one can assess the community opinion. Further, this method helps in measuring the community opinion towards functioning of continuing education centres.

(b) Development of Tool

A list of community representatives opinion were gathered from different sources like personal interviews with the community members, continuing education centre committee members, experts in the field and review of related literature. The items pooled were again rewritten for removing the ambiguous items, items without clarity, repetition and inaccuracies. The list thus prepared was presented to a panel of 5 experts and their suggestions were carried out. At this stage, there were 55 items in the community attitude scale.

(c) Rating Procedure

Before conducting the pilot study, the rating procedure was determined. Various types of rating methods viz., popular numerical rating scale consisting of five descriptive cues was chosen. The five descriptive cues viz., strongly agree, agree, undecided, disagree, strongly disagree were found to be more appropriate for rating the items chosen for the community opinion scale. The respondents were supposed to agree with any one of the alternative cues to mark the level of opinion possessed by the community towards various activities on the performance of preraks in continuing education centers.

(d) Pilot Study

Appropriate sample for pilot study was the community representatives. A sample of 120 villagers was selected at random from different continuing education centers in Nellore District of Andhra Pradesh. Care was also taken to see that the sample of villagers chosen represented different socio-economic status and different age groups. Items in the opinion scale were read out to the villagers and the responses given by them were noted down.

(e) Selection of Items

In order to determine the discriminative power and usefulness of statements chosen for the scale, the 't' value for each of the items was calculated as per the procedure suggested by Edwards, (1969). Items that had 't' value equal to or greater than 1.96 were selected for inclusion in the final form and all other items with 't' values less than 1.96 were discarded. Based on this procedure, 10 items were discarded. Thus, out of 55 items 45 were selected.

(f) Reliability of the Tool

For the purpose of the present scale, Test, re-test reliability was adopted to examine the reliability of the scale. This was done by obtaining the ratings for the scale with an interval of one month between the first and second administration of the scale to the same set of 120 community representatives. The correlation coefficient between the two administrations was 0.92 and was significant at 0.01 level. Hence, the opinion scale was considered to be highly reliable.

(g) Validity of the Scale

The present attitude scale developed on the lines described above has satisfactory validity with reference to the content, items and intrinsic validity. The description of details relating to the validity of the scale is as follows:

(i) **Content Validity:** Content validity indicates how adequate is the content of a test-sampling the domain about which inferences are to be made. Further, when taken collectively the items should constitute representative sample of the variable that is measured. The present attitude scale was developed keeping the above in view, as already described items for the scale were collected from different sources viz., neo-literates, preraks, Mandal Literacy Organizers (MLOs) and Supervisors. Further, they were also supplemented by a review of related literature and also by interviewing selected programme functionaries and experts to make sure that all possible items were included. Thus, it can be reasonable to assume that the instrument has satisfactory content validity.

(ii) **Item Validity:** Item validity stresses the extent to which the item predicts segregation of sample into those with low criterion scores. The discriminative power of each of the present scale was established by calculating their 't' values. Thus, the items chosen for both parts of the scale were found to be effectively valid.

(iii) **Intrinsic Validity:** Intrinsic validity indicates the degree to which a test measures what it purport to measure. This can also be stated as how well the obtained scores measures the tests true score component. Square root of the reliability value of the scale means its intrinsic validity. Thus, the intrinsic validity of the attitude scale was $\sqrt{0.92} = 0.96$ which can be assumed that the score has highly satisfying intrinsic validity.

(h) Brief Description of the Community opinion Scale

The final form of the community opinion scale developed in the lines described above consisted of 45 items. Each item can be rated on any of the 5 response category namely strongly agree, agree, undecided, disagree and strongly disagree which carried numerical values 5, 4, 3, 2 and 1 respectively. The score on the scale will range between 45 and 225 points.

LOCALE AND SAMPLE OF THE STUDY

To study of the functioning of continuing education centres in Nellore District of Andhra Pradesh was selected. The Nellore district consists of 3 Revenue Divisions i.e., Kavali, Nellore and Gudur. All the three divisions put together have 46 Revenue Mandals. A total of 356 continuing education centres are functioning in the district under the supervision of Zilla Saksharatha Samithi. From each of the Revenue division, 5 mandals were selected at random as a sample in the first stage. From the selected mandals, 40 continuing education centres were selected. All the preraks from each of the selected centre were interviewed. 3 neo-literates from each of the selected centre and 3 community representatives from the villages with continuing education centre were selected randomly.

The sample frame of the study are as follows:

Preraks (120)

Neo-literates (3 × 120) | Community Representatives (3 × 120)

District	-	1
Divisions	-	3
Mandals	-	15
Centres	-	120
Neo-literates	-	360
Community Representatives	-	360

DATA COLLECTION

The researcher visited all the centres selected for the study and established good rapport with neo-literates, preraks and community representatives. The performance and problem inventory schedule were administered to the preraks individually. The achievement test in literacy and the schedule to know the problems were administered to the selected neo-literates individually. The community opinion schedule on the performance of preraks in organising the continuing education centres was also administered to the community members individually. If tool approximately 2 hours for preraks, 2½ hours for neo-literates and 1½ hours for the community members for the completion of their representing tools.

ANALYSIS OF THE DATA

The data thus collected were pooled together and analysed by using chi-test and 't' test. ANOVA test developing upon the suitability of the tests to test the hypothesis formulated was utilised to draw inferences. The Chi-test was applied to find out the association between the selected socio-economic and demographic characteristics and neo-literates and preraks effectiveness. The 'F' or 't' test was applied to find out the differences if any between the mean performance/problem scores obtained by any two groups. Whereas, the ANOVA techniques were utilised to find out the difference amongst three or more groups.

5

ANALYSIS OF THE DATA AND INTERPRETATION OF THE RESULTS

The impact of literacy and adult education programmes clearly shows that in future, skill development and consequent increased economic opportunities must form one of the major components of initiatives in this area. The Government of India launched the National Literacy Mission (NLM, 1988) to empower the vast masses of illiterates not only to accelerate socio-economic development but also to improve the quality of human resources through the provision of opportunities to acquire literacy, social awareness and functional information. In order to realise this objective NLM has sponsored Total Literacy Campaigns (TLC) at district level to cover a large number of illiterates in a fixed time frame by adopting the strategy of area-specific, time-bound, cost-effective, out-come oriented and voluntarism.

The Zilla Saksharatha Samithi of Nellore District of Andhra Pradesh is implementing the Total Literacy Campaign in the name of 'Akshara Deepam' programme for the eradication of illiteracy in the age group of 9-35 years. Presently, the programme has entered the third phase i.e., continuing education stage for neo-literates after the completion of literacy and post-literacy stages. The continuing education centres follow an area-specific and community based approach. Continuing education centres are run by full-time facilitators or preraks who are drawn from the community itself. The continuing education centre serve as: library and reading room, teaching-learning centre, vocational training centre, a place for charcha mandal, a centre for conducting sports, games, recreational and cultural activities and also act as a information window and communication centre. The efficiency of the continuing education centre lies on the effective performance of various roles by the prerak. Prerak is the actual doers of the continuing education programme and a key element for the successful organisation of the continuing education centres at the grassroot level. Prerak has to interact with neo-literates at the field level and programme administrators at the apex level. Prerak has to be free from problems of all kinds, he/she has to be successful in performing various roles. Keeping in view, the importance of the prerak and his/her ability in overcoming the problems, it is essential to equip the preraks with the knowledge and skill in anticipating filed and organisational problems and in tackling them as and when they arise. In view of this, the present study is formulated to study the functioning of continuing education centres and the performance and problems of the preraks and neo-literates in Nellore District. The study is formulated with the following objectives.

Principal Objective

- To study the performance of the continuing education centres with special reference to preraks and neo-literates.

Subsidiary Objectives

- To identify the problems of the continuing education centres with special reference to preraks and neo-literates.
- To study the relationship amongst performance, problems and socio-economic and demographic characteristics of the preraks.
- To study the relationship amongst performance, problems and socio-economic and demographic characteristics of the neo-literates.
- To assess the community opinion towards the functioning of continuing education centres.

In the light of above objectives, the findings of the study are analysed in six sections. Section 1 measure the performance of preraks in organising continuing education centres and classify their performance as high level, medium level and low level performance. The association between the socio-economic and demographic characteristics of the preraks and their relationship with performance is presented. Identifies the problems of the preraks in organising continuing education centres and classify them as more prominent problems, prominent problems and less prominent problems of the preraks. The association between the socio-economic and demographic characteristics of the preraks and the problems encountered by them and their relationship with problems is presented in section 2. The level of performance of the neo-literates, and its association with socio-economic and demographic characteristics and their relationship with performance is presented in section 3. Identifies the problems of the neo-literates in attending continuing education centres and classify them as more prominent problems, prominent problems and less prominent problems of the neo-literates and its association with socio-economic and demographic characteristics and their relationship with problems is presented in section 4. Community representatives opinion (positive and negative) on the performance of preraks and relationship between the positive and negative opinions of the community representatives is presented in section 5. Section 6 describes the relationship between performance and problems of the preraks and neo-literates their relationship with preraks performance and community representatives opinions is presented.

CLASSIFICATION OF THE PERFORMANCE OF THE PRERAKS

In order to measure the performance of the preraks in organising the continuing education centres, a 5-point rating scale was administered to them. In order to categorise the preraks based on their performance, the method of mean ±½ standard deviation was followed and the performance of the preraks is categorised as high, medium and low level performance, i.e., the items having 326.41 and less mean were taken as low level performance, the mean values between

326.42 to 370.95 are taken as medium level performance and the items mean 370.96 and above are rated as high level performance. As per this classification, out of the 45 functions, preraks performance is very high on 13 items, in 18 items their performance is medium. On the remaining 14 items, their performance is very low. In other words, 40 per cent of the items are found to be medium level performance. The detailed discussion on the three level of performance of the preraks is discussed below.

Table 5.1: High level Performance and their respective Mean values checked by the Preraks

Sl. No.	*High level Performance*	*Mean Value*
1.	Literacy awareness campaigns through kalajathas, street plays, dances and slogans.	455.00
2.	Organising cycle rallies in the village.	453.00
3.	Discussion about the social evils and dowry.	438.00
4.	Creating awareness about folk arts among the neo-literates.	409.00
5.	Organisation of discussion groups (drinking water, health, diseases and traffic rules).	402.00
6.	Discussion about population, family planning and pollution.	401.00
7.	Participation in the review meetings and training programmes.	397.00
8.	Motivating the neo-literates to participate in games and sports.	390.00
9.	Organising singing competition.	386.00
10.	Seeking help from Mandal Literacy Oraganisers and supervisors in organising the continuing education centre activities.	381.00
11.	Forwarding different types of reports to nodal prerak.	378.00
12.	Recording information about the village.	374.00
13.	Maintaining records and registers in the centre.	374.00

(a) High level Performance

The purpose of identifying the high level performance of the preraks working in continuing education centres is to provide feedback to the programme advisors. The high level performance is noticed in the following spheres.

From the above Table 5.1, it is clear that out of 45 functions, in 13 activities preraks performance was of high quality. A glance at the above list clearly shows that out of the 13 items, 4 items come under recreational and cultural activities i.e., organising literacy awareness through kalajathas, street plays, dances, slogans, cycle rallies, folk arts and singing competitions to motivate the neo-literates. On the other hand 3 items belong to the organisation of discussions on safe drinking water, health and diseases, traffic rules, social evils, dowry, population, family planning and pollution. The rest of the activities coming under high level performance are participation in games and sports, seeking help from MLOs and supervisors in organising continuing education centre activities, forwarding different types of reports to Nodal preraks, gathering information about the village and maintaining records and registers in the centre.

(b) Medium level Performance

The Table 5.2 clearly indicates that out of the 45 functions, 18 items are found to be of medium level performance. 40 per cent of the preraks are discharging their functions at moderate level in organising the continuing education centres. Out of the 18 items, 3 items come under the organisation of group discussion namely facilitating the neo-literates participation, discussion about individual and village issues and individual development of the neo-literates. Running the library and reading room, supplying daily newspapers and monthly magazines, improving the literacy skills in evening classes, identifying the learning needs, conducting the sports and games competitions, teaching the importance of the sports and games, collection of the corpus fund through village education committees, creating awareness about DWCRA, CMEY, TRYSEM and DEEPAM

Table 5.2: Medium level performance and their respective Mean values checked by the Preraks

Sl. No.	*Medium level Performance*	*Mean Value*
1.	Supply of daily newspapers, fortnight and monthly magazines to the centre.	367.00
2.	Conducting sports and games competitions.	366.00
3.	Collection of corpus fund through village education committees.	366.00
4.	Facilitating neo-literate participation in group discussion.	364.00
5.	Creating awareness about DWCRA, CMEY, TRYSEM and DEEPAM.	360.00
6.	Evaluating the progress of the centre.	358.00
7.	Providing minimum facilities to the neo-literates.	355.00
8.	Discussion about individual and village issues.	342.00
9.	Organising short-term training programmes (leadership qualities, right to vote, agriculture, embroidery and tailoring).	342.00
10.	Improving literacy skills of neo-literates in the evening classes.	340.00
11.	Running the library and reading room.	339.00
12.	Collection of information about developmental programmes.	339.00
13.	Identification of learning needs of the neo-literates and preparing a plan to meet these needs.	337.00
14.	Organising continuing education centre programmes through village education committees.	336.00
15.	Arranging audio-visual aids.	333.00
16.	Discussion about individual development of the neo-literates.	332.00
17.	Organising quality of life improvement programmes.	330.00
18.	Making aware of the importance of the games and sports to neo-literates	330.00

programmes and arranged literacy are the activities falling under medium level performance.

One of the most important roles of the preraks is to evaluate the progress of the centre in terms of neo-literates performance, their retention skills and the training received and skill development programmes. Preraks experienced difficulty in organising the centres successfully due to lack of suitable facilities to organise short term training programmes. Preraks failed to collect the information about the developmental programmes and village education committees lacked interest to look into the programmes. Lack of audio-visual aids reduced the efficiency in the functioning of the centres.

Preraks should be trained properly in the methods to understand the socio-economic and personal background of the neo-literates, the ways and means of helping the participants to overcome their personal and village problems to improve the literacy skills among the neo-literates. In addition, the preraks should run the library and reading room and arrange the learning materials and also provide sports materials to the neo-literates. Preraks should be made to concentrate on short term training programmes to enhance the quality of human resources. All the continuing education centres should be given minimum facilities both for the preraks and the neo-literates.

(c) Low level Performance

From Table 5.3, out of the total 45 functions, in 14 functions preraks performance fall in the low category. Nearly one third of the preraks are performing at low level in organising the continuing education centres. The performance of the preraks is low in the areas of running the library and reading room i.e., lack of funds to organise the library, lack of books related to social, scientific, art and history. On the other hand, 3 items come under the area of continuing education programmes i.e., preraks did not organise equivalency programmes, self-employment programmes and vocational training programmes. Other low performance areas

Table 5.3: Low level performance and their respective Mean values checked by the Preraks

S.. No.	*Low level Performance*	*Mean Value*
1.	Running the information centre.	326.00
2.	Collection of funds and books to organise the library.	321.00
3.	Running the centre for six days in a week.	318.00
4.	Collecting books related to social, scientific, art and history.	317.00
5.	Organising the equivalency programmes.	316.00
6.	Creating conducive educational environment in the centre.	307.00
7.	Creating awareness about the utility of games and sports.	306.00
8.	Keeping records in continuing education centres about literacy and illiteracy.	306.00
9.	Organising cultural programmes with the help of local cultural troops.	304.00
10.	Organising development activities as per the individuals desire.	300.00
11.	Organising self-employment programmes.	294.00
12.	Organising recreational activities.	282.00
13.	Helping the self-help groups to acquire literacy.	280.00
14.	Organising vocational training programmes	240.00

are inability to provide information at the centre,. lack of educational environment, insufficient sports materials, getting co-operation from the local cultural troops, improper recreational activities and less participation of self-help groups in continuing education centres. In other words, this high risk group, if not tackled properly, may lead to the failure of the programme in all its fronts. So, the district administration has to concentrate on low and medium performing aspects of preraks through training and guidance.

Table 5.4: Mean Performance scores, SDs obtained by the Preraks of three groups and 'F' Value

Sl. No.	*Groups*	*N*	*Mean*	*S.D.*	*F*
1.	High level	38	136.57	4.20	
2.	Medium level	42	126.42	2.28	229.20**
3.	Low level	40	117.90	3.31	

** Significant at 0.01 level

Table 5.4 clearly indicates that nearly one third of the preraks are performing their function of organising the continuing education centres for the upliftment of literacy and continuing education programmes at high level. On the other hand, 35 per cent of the preraks are discharging their functions at medium level. Surprisingly, one third of the preraks are performing their functions at low level. In other words, this high risk group if not tackled properly, may lead to the failure of the programmes in all fronts. Further, the calculated 'F' value describes that there is a significant difference among the three groups of preraks in terms of their mean scores. Hence, the hypothesis "the level of the performance of preraks working in continuing education centres is not similar" is accepted.

(i) Performance of the Preraks

Recognising the relationship between literacy and economic development, the literacy promotion programmes are conceived and implemented throughout the country. Prerak is the key figure in the implementation of continuing education programme. Hence, the performance of the prerak is pivotal in achieving the objectives of the continuing education programme. The performance of the prerak also depends on the community support, personal characteristics of the prerak and his/her exposure to training, interest and aptitude for the job. Being a grass root level functionary, he/she has to interact with neo-literates at the field level and programme administrators at the apex level.

PERFORMANCE OF PRERAKS

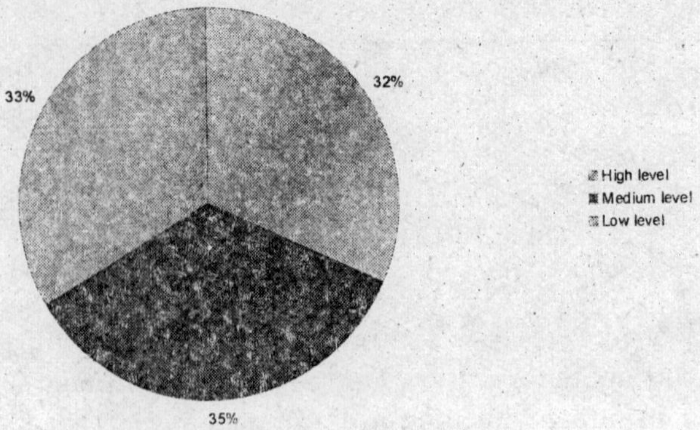

In other words, the prerak shoulders the sole responsibility of imparting literacy skills and organise training programmes to neo-literates in continuing education centres. The success or failure of continuing education centre always is attributed to the preraks efficiency or inefficiency. Since, the target group is poor people, preraks face a number of problems at the field level. In other words among the various factors, the personal characteristics and field problems affect the performance of the prerak. Prerak should not only a good teacher and organiser but also a good motivator and administrator besides having empathy towards the neo-literates. In addition, he/she should have the capacity to understand the problems of neo-literates and strive to solve them.

(ii) Preraks Performance V/s Socio-economic and Demographic Characteristics

(a) Association between Socio-economic and Demographic Characteristics and Performance

The continuing education programme is conceived for neo-literates, semi-literates, dropouts of the Total Literacy Campaign/Post-Literacy Campaign, pass outs of primary schools and all other members of the community and the new entrants in the age group of 9-35 years. In order to cover this large segment of the population, a large number of preraks are recruited from among the instructors/monitors already working in the TLC/PLC and also the educated youth who have come forward to render their services as preraks. In view of the large requirement almost all the individuals who offered their services are selected as preraks. As a result, individuals with different socio-economic backgrounds are involved in the programme as preraks. No doubt, the performance of the preraks also depends on their personal characteristics. In order to understand the association between socio-economic and demographic characteristics and the preraks performance, the data were analysed by categorising the sample into three groups based on their performance as low, moderate and more and correlated with the characteristics of the sample preraks and is subjected to chi-square test. The findings of the analysis are presented in table 5.5.

The results presented in Table 5.5 demonstrates that there is a significant association between socio-economic and demographic characteristics of the preraks viz., sex, marital status, age and number of children of the preraks and their performance. Hence, the hypothesis, "there is no significant association between the socio-economic and demographic characteristics and performance of the preraks working in continuing education centres" is not accepted in the case of the above variables and accepted in the case of other variables. In other words, while choosing the preraks, the above characteristics may be kept in view. On the other hand, the association is not significant in the case of caste, education, experience, occupation, income and type of family.

The above analysis only shows that there association between the personal variables and performance, but, the analysis is not sufficient to identify the characteristics which are contributing towards the preraks higher performance or otherwise. Hence, in order to delineate the characteristics contributing or not contributing to the performance of the preraks, further analysis is carried out by classifying the preraks into different groups based on the characteristics and by calculating their respective mean performance scores.

Table 5.5: Distribution of Chi-square Values in respect of Socio-economic and Demographic Characteristics of the Preraks in their Performance

Sl. No.	*Variable*	*Groups*	*N*	*D.F.*	χ^2
1.	Sex	Men	84	2	25.93**
		Women	36		
2.	Marital status	Married	82	2	26.14**
		Unmarried	38		
3.	Age	15-24	50		
		25-34	45	4	14.02**
		35+	25		
4.	Caste	SC/ST	50		
		BC	40	4	7.32@
		OC	30		
5.	Education	SSC	56		
		Inter	40	4	9.21@
		Degree	24		
6.	Experience	<2 years (less)	38	2	1.81@
		3 and above (more)	82		
7.	Occupation	Agriculture Labour	60		
		Agriculture	34	4	1.54@
		Employee	26		
8.	Income	<10,000 (less)	54	2	0.91@
		10,001-20,000 (more)	66		
9.	Number of children	No child	38		
		One	46	4	18.70**
		2 and more	36		
10.	Type of family	Nuclear	84	2	0.30@
		Joint	36		

@ Not significant * Significant at 0.05 level ** Significant at 0.01 level

(iii) Relationship between Socio-economic and Demographic Characteristics and Performance of the Preraks

In order to study the influence of the socio-economic and demographic characteristics of the preraks on their performance, the preraks were categorised into different groups based on their socio-economic and demographic characteristics and mean differences between them were identified. The Table 5.6 shows the mean performance scores, S.Ds obtained by the preraks belonging to different groups and the t/F values.

Table 5.6: Mean Performance scores, S.Ds obtained by the Preraks belonging to different groups and their respective t/F values

Sl. No.	*Variable*	*Groups*	*N*	*Mean*	*D.F.*	*t/F*
1.	Sex	Men	84	144.83	18.71	5.04**
		Women	36	126.11	17.29	
2.	Marital Status	Married	82	146.63	19.66	7.57**
		Un-married	38	125.47	10.87	
3.	Age	15-24	50	132.20	18.30	
		25-34	45	145.53	19.91	7.02**
		35+	25	145.32	17.98	
4.	Caste	SC/ST	50	142.00	19.79	
		BC	40	142.25	21.33	2.16@
		OC	30	133.40	16.64	
5.	Education	SSC	56	134.71	18.47	
		Inter	40	148.10	18.59	5.70**
		Degree	24	138.50	21.04	
6.	Experience	<2 years (less)	38	141.68	17.35	0.70@
		3 years & above (more)	82	139.12	21.01	
7.	Occupation	Agriculture Labour	60	140.93	18.88	
		Agriculture	34	138.29	21.38	0.18@
		Employee	26	139.76	20.30	
8.	Income	< 10,000 (less)	54	138.92	17.37	0.51@
		10,001-20,000 (more)	66	140.75	21.81	
9.	Number of children	No child	38	127.94	13.69	
		One	46	145.87	19.55	11.76**
		2 and more	36	145.00	20.47	
10.	Type of Family	Nuclear	84	139.52	20.27	0.35@
		Joint	36	140.89	19.17	

@ Not significant * Significant at 0.05 level ** Significant at 0.01 level

INFLUENCE OF THE SOCIO-ECONOMIC AND DEMOGRAPHIC CHARACTERISTICS ON THE PERFORMANCE OF THE PRERAKS

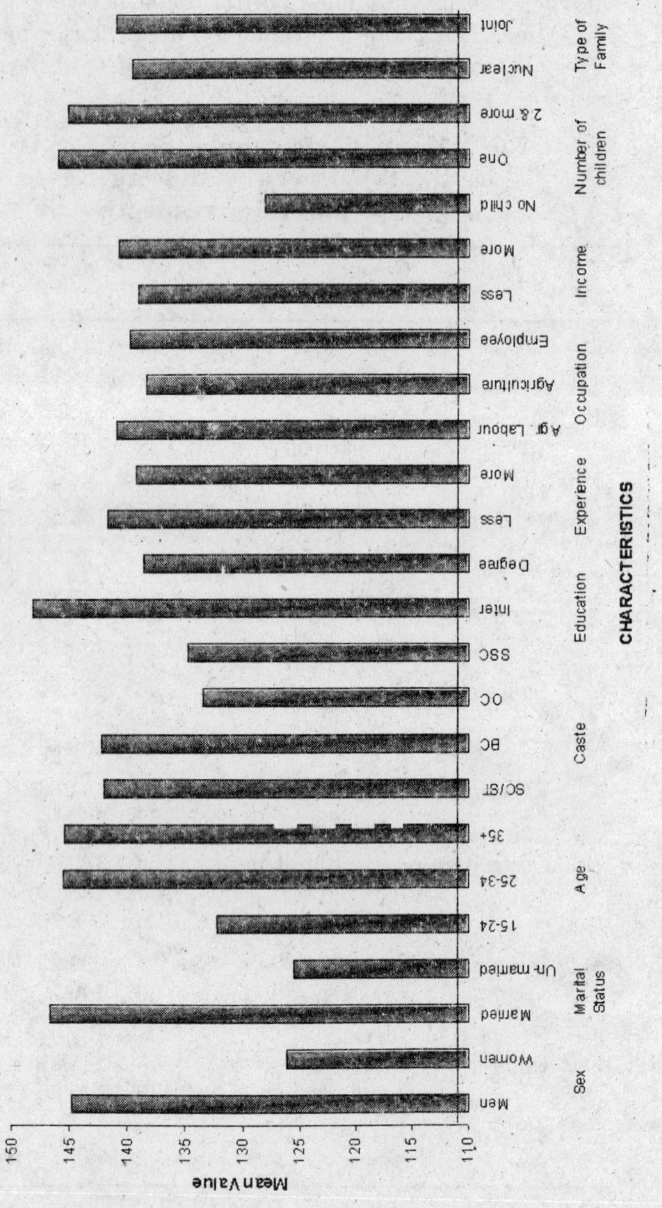

(a) Performance V/s Sex

In order to bring out the influence of the sex of the prerak on their performance, their respective mean performance scores were calculated and 't' test was applied to find out the significant difference if any between the two sexes. The result presented in the Table 5.6 indicates that men preraks have obtained better performance scores than their counterparts. In addition, the 't' test result shows that the obtained 't' value is more than the table value, indicating that the difference between mean performance is significant. Hence, while choosing the preraks for continuing education work, it is always safe to choose men as preraks so as to achieve better results and also to make the programme a success.

(b) Performance V/s Marital Status

In order to understand the influence of the marital status on the performance of the preraks, the preraks were categorised into two groups viz., married and unmarried. The performance scores of the married and unmarried are presented in the Table 5.6. The trend of the mean performance scores of the preraks shows that the married preraks have obtained better scores than the unmarried preraks. Further, the 't' test also shows that the difference between married and unmarried preraks is found significantly different from each other. Hence, while choosing the preraks only the married persons may be given priority.

(c) Performance V/s Age

In order to study the influence of age of preraks on their performance, preraks are categorised into three age groups viz., 15-24, 25-34 and 35 and above and their respective mean performance scores are calculated and 'F' values are applied to find out differences if any among the three age groups. The results presented in Table 5.6 indicates that the preraks falling in the age group 25-34 performed better than the other two groups. The preraks in the age group of 35 and above performed better than the 15-24 years age group. Further, it also shows that the differences between the mean performance scores of the preraks with different age groups are significant at 0.01 level. Hence, while selecting the preraks for continuing education work, it is always better to select preraks from 25-34 age group.

(d) Performance V/s Caste

Table 5.6 indicates that the difference between the obtained mean performance scores of the preraks belonging to SC/ST, BC and OC is not statistically significant. The trend of the mean performance scores shows that the preraks belonging to BC performed better than the other two groups. Among the other groups of preraks, the preraks belonging to SC/ST are found to be better than the OC.

(e) Performance V/s Education

In order to study the influence of education of preraks on their performance, the preraks are categorised into three groups viz., S.S.C., Inter and Degree. The trend of the mean performance scores shows that the preraks with 'Inter' education group are found to be popular in terms of their performance followed by Degree and S.S.C. In addition, the calculated 'F' value shows that the difference between the mean performance of the three groups of preraks is found to be significant at 0.01 level. The Inter qualified preraks seems to be most suitable to perform the task, may be they are able to reach to the level of neo-literates.

(f) Performance V/s Experience

Preraks chosen for the continuing education programme are from the group of preraks in Nellore District. In order to bring out the influence of the level of experience of the preraks in continuing education programme, they are categorised into two groups i.e., preraks with less experience and preraks with more experience. However, the trend of the mean performance scores presented in the Table 5.6 shows that the preraks with less experience are more effective than the preraks with more experience. This finding is puzzling and goes contrary to the experience and assumption. The calculated 't' value also shows that the difference is not significant.

(g) Performance V/s Occupation

Occupation wise preraks are grouped into three categories viz., agriculture labour, agriculture and employees. In order to understand the differential performance of the above groups of preraks, the mean performance scores are calculated and are presented in the Table 5.6. The trend of the mean performance scores presented in the Table illustrates that the preraks belonging to the occupation of agriculture labour performed better followed by employee and agriculture groups. In addition, the calculated 'F' value shows that the difference between the mean performance of the three groups of preraks was not found significantly.

(h) Performance V/s Income

Based on the level of income, the preraks are categorised into two groups viz., less income (less than Rs. 10,000/- per annum) and more income (more than Rs. 10,000/- per annum) and their performance scores are calculated and presented in the Table 5.6. The trend of the obtained mean performance scores shows the preraks with more income are found to more effective. However, the calculated 't' value is not significant. In other words, the performance of the preraks does not depend upon the income. Hence, while choosing the preraks their annual income need not to be taken into consideration.

(i) Performance V/s Number of Children

In order to find out the influence of the number of children possessed by the preraks on their performance, they are categorised into three groups those with no child, one child and two and more. The mean performance scores of the preraks belonging to the above groups are calculated and are presented in the Table 5.6. The result shows that the preraks having one child are found to be better performers than the other two groups. In addition, the results of the 'F' value indicates that there is a significant difference among the above three groups of preraks in their performance.

(j) Performance V/s Type of Family

The results presented in the Table-6 clearly shows that the influence of the type of family i.e., nuclear and joint families on the performance of the preraks. The trend of the mean performance scores obtained by the two groups of preraks i.e., nuclear and joint families clearly shows that the preraks from joint families have shown better performance than the preraks belonging to the nuclear family. However, the obtained 't' value is not significant. It shows that the type of family is not a significant predictor of the preraks performance.

In view of the above findings, the hypothesis "there is no significant influence of socio-economic and demographic characteristics and performance of the preraks working in continuing education centres" is accepted in the case of caste, experience, occupation, income and type of family and the hypothesis is not accepted in the case of sex, marital status, age, education and number of children.

Summing Up

From the above analysis, it is clear that the performance of the preraks is significantly influenced by the variables such as sex, marital status, age, education and number of children. The analysis also indicates that men, married, 25-34 age group, backward caste, inter educated, less experienced, agriculture labour, more income, one child and joint family preraks are found to be effective preraks working in continuing education centres. Steps should be taken to improve the performance of the counterpart groups.

CLASSIFICATION OF THE PROBLEMS OF THE PRERAKS

In order to identify the problems of the preraks in organising the continuing education centres, 5-point rating scale was used among the selected sample of preraks. In order to categorise the problems, the method of mean ±½ standard deviation was followed. The problems of the preraks are categorised as more prominent, prominent and less prominent i.e., the items having 326.57 and less mean are taken as less prominent problems, the mean values between 326.58 to 394.43 are taken as prominent problems and the items mean

394.44 and above are rated as more prominent problems. As per this categorisation, out of the 35 items, 10 items are found to be more prominent problems, 15 items are found to be prominent problems and 10 items as less prominent problems. Nearly 43 per cent of the problems are found to be prominent among the preraks in discharging their duties. The detailed discussion on the three categories of the problems of the preraks is discussed below.

(a) More Prominent Problems

The identified more prominent problems are as follows

Table 5.7: More Prominent Problems and their respective Mean values checked by the Preraks

Sl. No.	*More Prominent Problems*	*Mean Value*
1.	To collect corpus fund is difficult	496.00
2.	Preraks honorarium was not given in time.	484.00
3.	Dailies, weeklies, fortnightly and monthly magazines are not available in time in the centre.	478.00
4.	Unable to spend required time in teaching.	472.00
5.	Television, radio, tape recorders are not available in the centre.	432.00
6.	Men preraks organising the women neo-literate centres.	424.00
7.	No first aid box in the centre.	422.00
8.	Lack of basic facilities in the centre.	410.00
9.	Preraks are busy in performing other functions.	404.00
10.	Neo-literates are not co-operating with the preraks.	396.00

Table 5.7 clearly indicates that out of 35 items, 10 items are found to be more prominent problems. Prerak problems are categorised into two types i.e., personal and programme related problems. Out of the 10 problems, 7 items fall under programme related problems, the rest fall under personal category. Programme related problems are seven in number. They are collection of corpus fund, preraks honorarium is not

given in-time, dailies, weeklies, fortnightly and monthly magazines are not available in-time in the centre, lack of audio-visual aids, lack of minimum facilities at the centres and men preraks organising the women neo-literate centres. Personal problems are lack of time, attending to other functions and lack of co-operation from the neo-literates. A strategy must be worked out by both the administration and the preraks themselves to solve above mentioned problems.

(b) Prominent Problems

The second category of the problems i.e., prominent problems of the preraks identified are as follows:

Table 5.8: Prominent problems and their respective Mean values checked by the Preraks

Sl. No.	*Prominent Problems*	*Mean Value*
1.	No rewards and awards to the preraks for doing hard work.	394.00
2.	Attending to agriculture work.	392.00
3.	Mandal Parishad Development Officers are not supervising the centres.	388.00
4.	Lack of convincing approach by the preraks.	386.00
5.	Lack of co-operation from the Village Administrative Officers and Village Development Officers.	376.00
6.	Family problems of the preraks.	370.00
7.	Non co-operation from village educators.	368.00
8.	Inability of the preraks to understand the psychological problems of the neo-literates.	364.00
9.	No close interaction with the neo-literates.	356.00
10.	Non co-operation of preraks family members.	346.00
11.	Lack of registers and records.	346.00
12.	Lack of co-operation from the village leaders and village elders.	346.00
13.	Lack of experience as a volunteer.	344.00
14.	Age difference between neo-literates and preraks.	332.00
15.	Financial problems of the preraks.	330.00

From Table 5.8, it appears that out of 35 items, 15 items are found to be prominent problems of the preraks. Out of the 15 problems, 10 problems come under personal problems, remaining 5 items are programme related problems.

Prerak personal problems (10) are agricultural work, family problems, financial problems, non co-operation of family members and village educators, inability of the preraks to convince the neo-literates, inability of the preraks to understand the psychological problems of neo-literates, no close interaction with the neo-literates, age difference between neo-literates and preraks and lack of experience. Programme related problems of the prerak are no rewards and awards to the prerak, lack of co-operation from the VAOs, VDOs, village elders and village leaders and non-supervision of the centres by the MPDO's. In addition to the above, no support is forthcoming developmental departments.

LESS PROMINENT PROBLEMS

The third category of the problems i.e., less prominent problems of the preraks identified are as follows:

Table 5.9: Less prominent problems and their respective Mean values checked by the Preraks

Sl. No.	*Less Prominent Problems*	*Mean Value*
1.	Personal work of preraks.	324.00
2.	Inability of the preraks to run the centres.	312.00
3.	Lack of qualifications.	312.00
4.	Lack of co-operation from the Mandal Literacy Organisers and supervisors.	312.00
5.	Lack of black boards, books and notice boards etc., in the centre.	296.00
6.	Non-completion of the primers in time.	290.00
7.	Lack of co-operation from the continuing education centre chairman, ward members and sarpanch.	278.00
8.	No value to the certificates given by the prerak.	248.00
9.	Lack of books for the neo-literates.	210.00
10.	Inadequate training of the preraks.	206.00

From Table 5.9, out of the 35 problems, 10 items are found to be less prominent. Out of this, 5 items come under prerak personal problems, remaining 5 items fall under programme related problems. Personal problems of the preraks (5) are personal works, lack of qualifications, inability of the preraks to organise the centres, non-completion of primers in time and no value to the certificates given by the preraks. Programme related problems of the preraks are lack of co-operation from the mandal literacy organisers, supervisors, CEC Chairman, sarpanch, ward members, lack of teaching-learning materials and inadequate training of the preraks.

Table 5.10: Mean Problem scores, SDs obtained by the Preraks of three groups and 'F' value

Sl. No.	*Groups*	*N*	*Mean*	*S.D.*	*F*
1.	More prominent problems	38	115.00	3.55	
2.	Prominent problems	50	104.44	2.21	367.83**
3.	Less prominent problems	32	95.37	3.31	

** Significant at 0.01 level

The Table 5.10 clearly shows that one-fourth of the preraks are doing their functions smoothly in organising the continuing education centres. On the other hand, 42 per cent of the preraks are of the opinion that they are exposed to moderate problems in running the continuing education centres. Contrary to the above, one-third of the preraks are found to be facing more prominent problems in organising the continuing education centres. There is a possibility that because of the group facing more prominent problems, the programme may face many difficulties. Hence, appropriate measures should be taken to rectify the difficulties by organising intensive training programme to this group of preraks to overcome the problems at the initial stages. The above description clearly demonstrates that the intensity of problems faced by the preraks is not of similar intensity to all the preraks, each group feels it differently. Further, the calculated 'F' value shows that there is a significant difference among the three groups of preraks in terms of their mean problem scores. Hence, the hypothesis "the intensity of the problems encountered by the preraks, working in continuing education centres is not similar" is accepted.

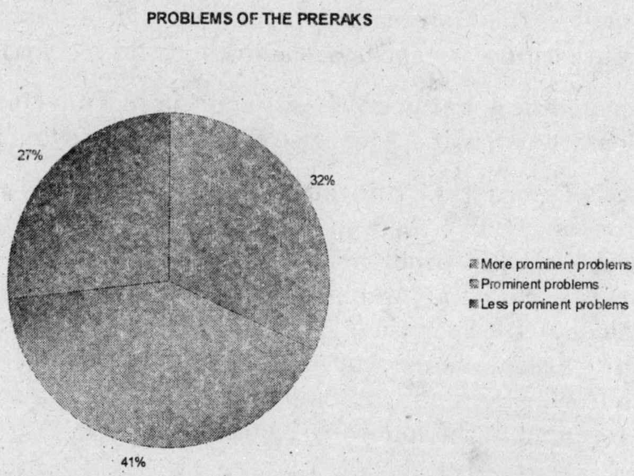

Table 5.11: Problem areas and respective Mean problem scores, S.Ds and 't' value (Preraks)

S. No.	*Problem Area*	*N*	*Mean*	*S.D.*	*'t'*
1.	Personal problems	120	56.91	5.75	12.39**
2.	Programme related problems	120	48.45	4.78	

** Significant at 0.01 level

The mean problem scores of two different problem areas of preraks i.e., personal problems and programme related problems and their respective mean problem scores and are calculated to find out the significant difference if any between the two problem areas. The results are presented in the above Table 5.11 demonstrates that personal problems are found to be more acute than the programme related problems. However, the calculated 't' test indicates that the difference is significant at 0.01 level. Hence, the hypothesis "there is no significant difference between the prerak personal problems and programme related problems" is not accepted. In view of the above, the programme planners and administrators should make a note of the above and help the preraks to overcome the problems faced by them in their day-to-day activities by equipping them through in-service and pre-service training. Further, the training curriculum should be restructured so as to incorporate above areas in the training curriculum.

Association between Socio-economic and Demographic Characteristics and Area wise Problems of the Preraks

In order to find out the association between socio-economic and demographic characteristics and problems of the preraks their problems are classified into two areas i.e., prerak personal and programme related problems were calculated as per their characteristics. In order to find out the association and relationship between preraks characteristics and problems further analysis is made and presented in the following pages.

(a) Association between Socio-economic and Demographic Characteristics and Personal Problems of the preraks

In order to understand the association between socio-economic and demographic characteristics and problems of the preraks are categorised into three groups based on their problems high, medium, low and correlated with the characteristics of the sample preraks and is subjected to chi-square test. The findings are presented in the Table 5.12.

According to the Table 5.12, there is significant association with the type of family of the preraks. On the other hand, association is not significant in the case of sex, marital status, age, caste, education, experience, occupation, income and number of children. Hence, the hypothesis "there is no significant association between the socio-economic and demographic characteristics and personal problems encountered by the preraks in organising the continuing education centres" is not accepted in the case of type of family and hypothesis is accepted in the case of the rest of the variables.

Table 5.12: Distribution of Chi-square values in respect of the Socio-economic and Demographic Characteristics of the Preraks in the Problem Area of Personal Problems

Sl. No.	*Variable*	*D.F.*	χ^2
1.	Sex	2	5.37@
2.	Marital Status	2	4.32@
3.	Age	4	8.95@
4.	Caste	4	6.70@
5.	Education	4	7.63@
6.	Experience	2	3.99@
7.	Occupation	4	1.07@
8.	Income	2	0.5@
9.	Number of Children	4	5.17@
10.	Type of Family	2	10.55**

@ Not Significant ** Significant at 0.01 level.

(b) Relationship between Socio-economic and Demographic Characteristics and Problems of the Preraks in the area of Personal Problems

In order to find out the relationship between socio-economic and demographic characteristics and problems in the area of prerak personal problems, preraks are categorised into different groups based on their socio-economic and demographic characteristics. The mean problem scores are calculated for all the groups. The t/F test was applied to find out the significant difference if any among different groups. The obtained results are presented in the Table 5.13.

As per the Table 5.13, the trend of the mean problem scores indicates that women preraks, married, 25-34 years age group, SC/ST, S.S.C. with more experience, agriculture as main occupation, more income, one child and joint family groups are facing more problems.. On the other hand, men preraks, unmarried preraks, 15-24 years age

Table 5.13: The Mean problem scores, SDs obtained by the Preraks belonging to different groups along with t/F values in the area of Personal Problems

Sl. No.	*Variable*	*Groups*	*N*	*Mean*	*S.D.*	*t/F*
1.	Sex	Men	84	56.16	5.65	2.23*
		Women	36	58.67	5.60	
2.	Marital Status	Married	82	57.80	5.96	2.77**
		Unmarried	38	55.00	4.73	
3.	Age	15-24	50	55.52	4.82	
		25-34	45	58.31	6.33	2.89@
		35+	25	57.20	5.70	
4.	Caste	SC/ST	50	57.54	6.01	
		BC	40	56.35	5.40	0.51@
		OC	30	56.63	5.66	
5.	Education	SSC	56	58.25	5.21	
		Inter	40	54.77	4.95	4.57*
		Degree	24	57.37	7.01	
6.	Experience	<2 years (Less)	38	56.47	5.34	0.59@
		3 and above (More)	82	57.12	5.92	
7.	Occupation	Agriculture Labour	60	56.33	4.40	
		Agriculture	34	57.70	7.59	0.65@
		Employee	26	57.23	5.54	
8.	Income	< 10,000 (Less)	54	56.40	4.57	
		10,001 – 20,000/- (More)	66	57.33	6.53	0.91@
9.	Number of children	No child	38	55.21	4.59	
		One	46	58.78	6.45	4.48*
		2 and more	36	56.33	5.19	
10.	Type of Family	Nuclear	84	56.78	6.43	0.46@
		Joint	36	57.22	3.67	

@ Not Significant * Significant at 0.05 level ** Significant at 0.01 level.

group, B.C. with Inter qualification, less experience, agriculture labour, less income, no child and nuclear family have faced fewer problems.

The obtained t/F values show that there is a significant relationship between problems of the preraks in the area of prerak personal problems and socio-economic and demographic characteristics viz., sex, marital status, education and number of children. Hence, the hypothesis "there is no significant relationship between the socio-economic and demographic characteristics and the personal problems encountered by the preraks in organising the continuing education centres" is not accepted. However, the hypothesis is accepted in the case of the variables viz., age, caste, experience, occupation, income and type of family.

Table 5.14: Distribution of Chi-square values in respect of the Socio-economic Demographic Characteristics of the Preraks in the Problem Area of Programme related Problems

Sl. No.	*Variable*	*D.F.*	χ^2
1.	Sex	2	6.48*
2.	Marital Status	2	16.36**
3.	Age	4	11.05*
4.	Caste	4	10.20*
5.	Education	4	8.19@
6.	Experience	2	2.76@
7.	Occupation	4	14.86**
8.	Income	2	0.66@
9.	Number of Children	4	16.18**
10.	Type of Family	2	6.43*

@ Not Significant * Significant at 0.05 level ** Significant at 0.01 level.

In order to find out the association between the socio-economic and demographic characteristics and problem of the preraks in the area of programme related problems, the preraks are classified into different groups based on their socio-economic and demographic characteristics. The Chi-square test is applied and the findings are presented in the Table 5.14. The association is significant in the case of sex, marital status, age, caste, occupation, number of children and type of family. Hence, the hypothesis "there is no significant association between the socio-economic and demographic characteristics and the programme related problems encountered by the preraks in organising the continuing education centres" is not accepted. But, the association is not significant in the case of education, experience and income, hence, the hypothesis is accepted regarding these characteristics.

Table 5.15: Mean problem scores, SDs obtained by the Preraks belonging to different groups along with t/F values in the area of Programme related Problems

Sl. No.	*Variable*	*Groups*	*N*	*Mean*	*S.D.*	*t/F*
1.	Sex	Men	84	47.71	4.75	2.73**
		Women	36	50.16	4.40	
2.	Marital Status	Married	82	48.56	4.15	0.32@
		Unmarried	38	48.21	5.91	
3.	Age	15-24	50	49.72	5.56	
		25-34	45	47.91	3.84	3.50*
		35+	25	46.88	3.91	
4.	Caste	SC/ST	50	47.22	3.89	
		BC	40	51.10	4.96	10.62**
		OC	30	46.96	4.40	
5.	Education	SSC	56	49.10	4.93	
		Inter	40	47.95	4.63	0.99@
		Degree	24	47.75	4.49	
6.	Experience	<2 years (Less)	38	47.47	4.28	1.61@
		3 and above (More)	82	48.90	4.93	
7.	Occupation	Agriculture Labour	60	49.30	4.19	
		Agriculture	34	47.52	4.91	1.91@
		Employee	26	47.69	5.49	
8.	Income	< 10,000 (Less)	54	48.96	4.22	
		10,001 – 20,000/- (More)	66	48.03	5.16	1.08@
9.	Number of children	No child	38	48.57	5.73	
		One	46	49.17	4.19	1.42@
		2 and more	36	47.38	4.16	
10.	Type of Family	Nuclear	84	49.21	4.69	2.79**
		Joint	36	46.66	4.52	

@ Not Significant* Significant at 0.05 level** Significant at 0.01 level

The results presented in the Table 5.15 show that there is a significant difference among different groups of preraks based on sex, age, caste and type of family, hence the hypothesis "there is no significant relationship between the socio-economic and demographic characteristics and the programme related problems encountered by the preraks in organising the continuing education centres" is not accepted in the case of the above variables. In the case of other variables like marital status, education, experience, occupation, income and number of children, the difference between mean problem score is not significant. However, the trend of the mean problem scores of both the groups indicates that the men preraks, unmarried, 35 and more years age group, OC, Degree, less experience, agriculture, more income, two and more children and joint family are found to facing fewer problems comparatively than the other groups.

Table 5.16: Distribution of Chi-square values in respect of the Socio-economic and Demographic Characteristics of Preraks in Total Problems

Sl. No.	*Variable*	*D.F.*	χ^2
1.	Sex	2	17.95**
2.	Marital Status	2	8.11*
3.	Age	4	3.00@
4.	Caste	4	6.59@
5.	Education	4	14.91**
6.	Experience	2	4.14@
7.	Occupation	4	4.60@
8.	Income	2	1.84@
9.	Number of Children	4	8.51@
10.	Type of Family	2	2.33@

@ Not Significant * Significant at 0.05 level ** Significant at 0.01 level

The findings presented in the Table 5.16 illustrates that there is a significant association between the socio-economic and demographic characteristics viz., sex, marital status and education and their problems (total problems). Hence, the hypothesis "there is no significant association between socio-economic and demographic characteristics and the problems encountered by the preraks in organising the continuing education centres" is not accepted in the case of the above variables and accepted in the case of other variables viz., age, caste, experience, occupation, income, number of children and type of family as they do not have any association with their problems.

Table 5.17: Mean problem scores, SDs obtained by the Preraks belonging to different groups along with t/F values in Total Problems

Sl. No.	*Variable*	*Groups*	*N*	*Mean*	*S.D.*	*t/F*
1.	Sex	Men	84	103.88	7.86	3.26**
		Women	36	108.83	7.50	
2.	Marital Status	Married	82	106.36	7.30	1.86@
		Unmarried	38	103.21	9.18	
3.	Age	15-24	50	105.24	8.27	
		25-34	45	106.22	7.94	0.56@
		35+	25	104.08	7.75	
4.	Caste	SC/ST	50	104.76	7.84	
		BC	40	107.45	7.24	2.21@
		OC	30	103.60	8.89	
5.	Education	SSC	56	107.35	7.69	
		Inter	40	102.72	6.93	4.00*
		Degree	24	105.12	9.37	
6.	Experience	<2 years (Less)	38	103.94	7.50	1.36@
		3 and above (More)	82	106.02	8.25	
7.	Occupation	Agriculture Labour	60	105.63	6.77	
		Agriculture	34	105.23	10.12	0.07@
		Employee	26	104.92	7.83	
8.	Income	< 10,000 (Less)	54	105.37	6.78	
		10,001-20,000/- (More)	66	105.36	9.00	0.05@
9.	Number of children	No child	38	103.78	8.79	
		One	46	107.95	7.53	3.98*
		2 and more	36	103.72	7.04	
10.	Type of Family	Nuclear	84	106.00	8.58	1.47@
		Joint	36	103.88	6.53	

@ Not Significant* Significant at 0.05 level ** Significant at 0.01 level

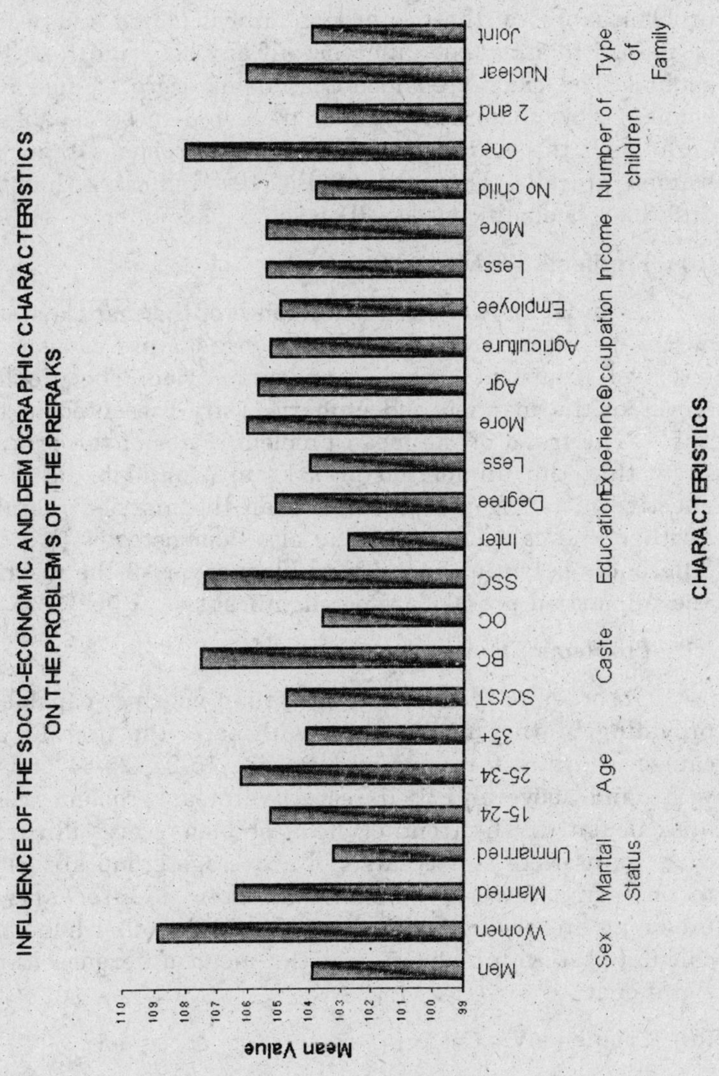
INFLUENCE OF THE SOCIO-ECONOMIC AND DEMOGRAPHIC CHARACTERISTICS
ON THE PROBLEMS OF THE PRERAKS
Mean Value
99
100
101
102
103
104
105
106
107
108
109
110
Men
Women
Married
Unmarried
15-24
25-34
35+
SC/ST
BC
OC
SSC
Inter
Degree
Less
More
Agr.
Agriculture
Employee
Less
More
No child
One
2 and
Nuclear
Joint
Sex
Marital Status
Age
Caste
Education
Experience
Occupation
Income
Number of children
Type of Family
CHARACTERISTICS

(a) Problems V/s Sex

In order to identify the group which is facing the problems relating to the organisation of centres, the mean problem scores of the two groups are calculated and 't' test is applied to study the differences if any between these two groups. The calculated mean problems score of men and women show that men preraks are found to be capable of organising the centres and faced fewer problems than the women preraks. The calculated 't' test indicates that the difference is significant at 0.01 level.

(b) Problems V/s Marital Status

In order to find out the influence of the marital status on the problems of the prerak, the preraks are categorised into two groups i.e., married and unmarried. The problem scores of the married and unmarried are presented in the Table. The trend of the mean problem scores of the preraks show that the unmarried preraks are found to be more effective in facing the problems than the married preraks. Further, the calculated 't' value also demonstrates that the differences between the mean problem scores of the married and unmarried preraks are not significant.

(c) Problems V/s Age

In order to identify the age group which is capable of providing literacy to illiterates with ease, the preraks are categorised into three age groups viz., 15-24, 25-34 and 35 years and above and their respective mean problem scores are calculated. The trend of mean problem scores illustrate that the preraks of 35 years and above age group are found to be facing fewer problems than their counterparts in providing literacy to the neo-literates. On the other hand, the calculated 't' value shows that the mean difference is not significant.

(d) Problems V/s Caste

The results relating to the problems of the preraks in relation to their caste shows that the OC group is found to be facing fewer problems than the SC/ST and BC groups. The calculated 'F' value indicates that the mean problem scores of all these three categories are not significantly different from each other.

(e) Problems V/s Education

As the preraks are drawn from various walks of life, they differ in their level of education. In order to understand the influence of education on the problems of the prerak, the preraks are categorised into three groups on the basis of their level of education i.e., S.S.C., Inter and Degree. The trend of the mean problems scores illustrate that 'Inter' educated preraks are found to be more effective in facing the problems than the Degree and SSC educated preraks. Further, the calculated 'F' value also shows that the difference between the mean problem scores of SSC, Inter and Degree preraks are found to be significant at 0.05 level.

(f) Problems V/s Experience

In order to understand the influence of experience on problem facing capabilities, the preraks are categorised into less experienced (less than two years) and more experience (more than two years). The trend of the mean problem scores reveal that the less experienced are found to be facing fewer problems than the more experienced preraks. Further, the calculated 't' value also shows that the difference between these two groups is not significant. This is one interesting finding which goes against the general assumption that experience gives capacity to face the problems than the other way.

(g) Problems V/s Occupation

With regard to the problems versus occupation, the trend of the mean problem scores show that the preraks who are employed faced fewer problems than the other preraks belonging to the occupation of labour and agriculture. No doubt, the preraks with the background of employment proved to be effective in terms of the problems faced by them but their overall proportion is less. However, the calculated 'F' value shows that there is no significant difference between the mean problem scores of the preraks belonging to different occupational groups.

(h) Problems V/s Income

In order to find out the influence of the income of the preraks on their problem facing capabilities, the sample preraks are categorised into two groups i.e., less income group (less than Rs. 10,000 per annum) and more income group (more than Rs. 10,000 per annum). The mean problem scores of these two groups are calculated and 't' test is applied to find out the difference if any between the two mean problem scores. The obtained mean problem score and 't' value illustrates that there is no significant difference between the preraks with less income and more income groups. It may be said that, the two groups are facing similar problems.

(i) Problems V/s Number of Children

For analysing the influence of the children on the problems faced by the preraks in organising the continuing education centres, preraks are classified into three groups viz., preraks with no children, one child and two and more children. The problem mean scores of the preraks of the three groups shows that the preraks with two and more children are found to be facing fewer problems followed by preraks with no child and one child. Preraks with more children are capable of organising the centre effectively and also in solving the problems than other groups. Probably, they have carried their domestic experience of tackling the children to the continuing education centres in solving their problems. The 'F' value shows that there is a significant difference among the three groups of preraks with difference in number of children.

(j) Problems V/s Type of Family

In order to find out the influence of the type of family of the preraks on the extent of the problems faced by them, the preraks are categorised as per their type of family i.e., nuclear and joint family. As per this classification, there are 84 preraks with nuclear family background and 36 with joint family background. The mean problem score of these two categories of preraks shows that the preraks with joint family background are found to be facing fewer problems than the preraks with nuclear family background. The calculated 't' value shows that the mean difference between these two types of preraks is not statistically significant.

Keeping in view of the above results, the null hypothesis "there is no significant relationship between the socio-economic and demographic characteristics and the problems encountered by the preraks in organising the continuing education centres" is accepted in case of marital status, age, caste, experience, occupation, income and type of family and the hypothesis is not accepted in case of sex, education and number of children.

SUMMING UP

From the above analysis, it appears that men preraks, unmarried preraks, 35 and above years age, other community, Inter educated, less experience, employees, more income, two and more children and joint family groups are found to be facing fewer problems in organising the continuing education centres. Contrary to the above women preraks, married preraks, 25-34 years age group, Backward Caste, S.S.C. educated, more experience, agriculture labour, less income, one child and nuclear family are found to be facing more number of problems in organising continuing education centres. It would be rewarding to identify the reasons for poor performance of the various groups so that their performance can be enhanced.

CLASSIFICATION OF THE PERFORMANCE OF THE NEO-LITERATES

(i) Performance of the Neo-literates

In order to measure the performance of the neo-literates attending the continuing education centres, an achievement test in literacy intended to estimate the level of attainment in reading, writing and arithmetic skills–3R's is administered to the neo-literates in continuing education centres. As per the National Literacy Mission norm, to declare a person as literate he/she has to obtain 50 per cent of marks in each of the three components and 70 per cent as an aggregate. The above criteria is adopted to arrive at literacy attainment rate among the neo-literates of the continuing education programme.

Neo-literate is a basic person of the continuing education programme. The success or failure of the programme largely depend upon the neo-literates participation, involvement, co-operation, co-ordination, unity, literacy skills and availability of information on developmental programmes. Literacy is a crucial input for economic and socio-cultural change. In this section, an attempt is made to find out the level of performance of the neo-literates and association between performance of neo-literates and socio-economic and demographic characteristics of the neo-literates.

Table 5.18: Mean performance scores, SDs obtained by the Neo-literates of three groups and 'F' values

Sl. No.	*Groups*	*N*	*Mean*	*S.D.*	*F*
1.	High level	195	74.41	4.75	664.83**
2.	Medium level	143	61.53	5.26	
3.	Low level	22	35.63	8.15	

** Significant at 0.01 level

The Table 5.18 clearly shows that 54 per cent of the sample are reached as per NLM norms and obtained high level performance of the neo-literates. On the other hand, 40 per cent of the neo-literates are not reached the NLM norms. But, the above neo-literates are possessed the average marks i.e., 50-69 marks. Contrary to the above, 6 per cent of the neo-literates are having a less than 49 marks. In other words, these two groups i.e., medium and low level performance of the neo-literates are not attended the centres regularly, may lead to the failure of the programme in all fronts. Hence, appropriate measures should be taken to rectify the difficulties by organising the literacy classes and special training programmes to this group of neo-literates. Further, the calculated 'F' value shows that there is a significant

PERFORMANCE OF THE NEO-LITERATES

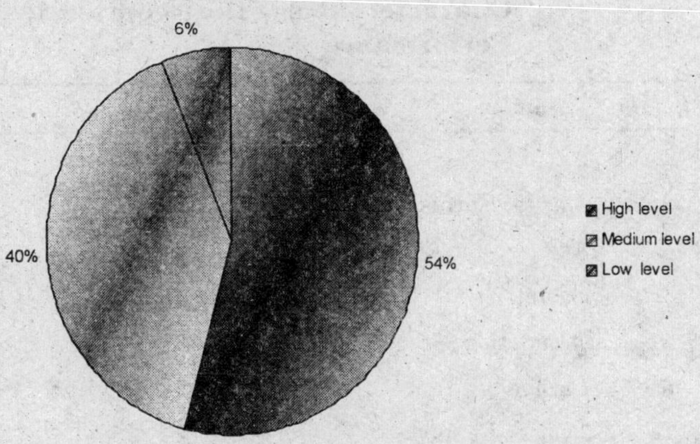

difference among the three groups of neo-literates in terms of their mean performance scores. Hence, the hypothesis "the level of performance of the neo-literates in attending the continuing education centres is not similar" is accepted.

(ii) Neo-literates Performance V/s Socio-economic and Demographic Characteristics

(a) Association between Socio-economic and Demographic Characteristics and Performance

The continuing education programme is conceived for neo-literates, semi-literates, dropouts of the TLC/PLC, all other members of the community and new entrants in the age group of 9-35 years. In order to understand the association between socio-economic and demographic characteristics and performance, data is analysed by categorising the sample into three groups based on their performance as high, medium and low. The level of performance is correlated with the characteristics of the sample. The data is subjected to chi-square test. The findings of the analysis is presented in the table 5.19.

The results presented in Table 5.19 indicates that there is a significant association between socio-economic and

Table 5.19: Distribution of Chi-square values in respect of the Socio-economic and Demographic Characteristics of the Neo-literates in their Performance

Sl. No.	*Variable*	*D.F.*	χ^2
1.	Sex	2	3.74@
2.	Marital Status	2	2.12@
3.	Age	4	11.58*
4.	Caste	4	3.96@
5.	Occupation	2	8.67*
6.	Income	2	1.36@
7.	Type of Family	2	3.11@
8.	Number of Children	4	3.12@

@ Not significant *Significant at 0.05 level

demographic characteristics of the neo-literates viz., age and occupation and performance of the neo-literates. Hence, the hypothesis, "There is no significant association between the socio-economic and demographic characteristics and performance of the neo-literates" is not accepted in the case of the above variables and accepted in the case of other variables. In other words, while selecting the neo-literates the above characteristics may be kept in view. On the other hand, the association is not significant in the case of sex, marital status, caste, income, type of family and number of children.

(iii) Relationship between Socio-economic and Demographic Characteristics and Performance of Neo-literates

In order to study the influence of the socio-economic and demographic characteristics of the neo-literates on their performance. Neo-literates are categorised into different groups based on their socio-economic and demographic characteristics and mean differences between them are identified. The Table 5.20 illustrates the mean performance scores, SDs obtained by the neo-literates belonging to different groups and the t/F values.

Table 5.20: Mean Performance scores, SDs obtained by the Neo-literates belonging to different groups and their respective t/F values

Sl. No.	*Variable*	*Groups*	*N*	*Mean*	*S.D.*	*t/F*
1.	Sex	Men	180	68.36	10.72	2.41*
		Women	180	65.49	11.78	
2.	Marital Status	Married	257	66.47	12.15	1.36@
		Unmarried	103	68.05	8.95	
3.	Age	15-24	149	67.87	10.15	4.12*
		25-34	136	64.79	11.43	
		35+	75	68.92	12.77	
4.	Caste	SC/ST	148	65.68	12.40	1.75@
		BC	114	68.29	10.90	
		OC	98	67.21	9.93	
5.	Occupation	Agriculture labour	255	65.81	12.30	3.47**
		Agriculture and others	105	69.62	8.03	
6.	Income	< 10,000 (Less)	221	66.55	11.65	0.79@
		10,001-20,000/- (More)	139	67.51	10.84	
7.	Type of Family	Nuclear	271	66.58	11.59	1.04@
		Joint	89	67.96	10.53	
8.	Number of children	No child	119	67.37	9.20	0.45@
		One	131	67.23	12.37	
		2 and above	110	66.07	12.13	

@ Not significant *Significant at 0.05 level **Significant at 0.01 level

(a) Performance V/s Sex

In order to find out the influence of the sex of the neo-literates on their performance, the neo-literates mens and womens respective mean performance scores are calculated and 't' test applied to find out the significant difference if any between the two sex groups. The results presented in the Table-20 illustrates that men neo-literates have obtained better performance scores than women neo-literates. In addition, the 't' test result shows that there is significant difference between mean performance.

INFLUENCE OF THE SOCIO-ECONOMIC AND DEMOGRAPHIC CHARACTERISTICS ON THE PERFORMANCE OF NEO-LITERATES

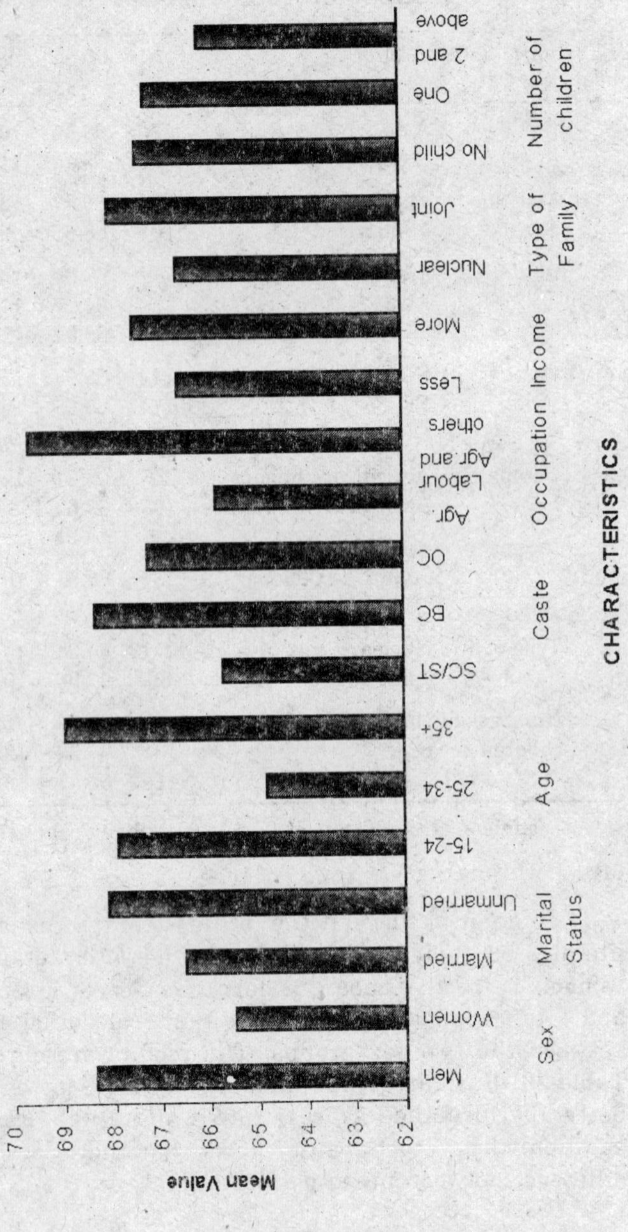

(b) Performance V/s Marital Status

In order to bring out the influence of the marital status on the performance of the neo-literates, the neo-literates are categorised into two groups viz., married and unmarried. The trend of the mean performance scores show that the unmarried neo-literates have obtained better scores than the married neo-literates. The 't' test also shows that the difference between married and unmarried neo-literates is not significantly different from each other.

(c) Performance V/s Age

In order to study the influence of the age of neo-literates on their performance, the neo-literates are categorised into three groups viz., 15-24, 25-34 and 35 and above years. The trend of the mean performance scores of the neo-literates illustrates that the 35 and above years performed better than the other two groups. The neo-literates in the age group of 15-24 performed better than the 25-34 years age group. In addition, the 'F' value also shows that the difference between the three groups of the neo-literates is found to be statistically significant.

(d) Performance V/s Caste

The Table 5.20 gives the details of the difference between the obtained mean performance scores of the neo-literates belonging to OC, BC and SC/ST is not statistically significant. The trend of the mean performance scores show that the neo-literates belonging to BC performed better than the other two groups. Among the other groups of neo-literates, the neo-literates belonging to OC are found to be better than the SC/ST. The above trend clearly demonstrates that BC group neo-literates are participating in the continuing education centre activities effectively when compared to other groups.

(e) Performance V/s Occupation

In order to bring out the influence of the occupation of the neo-literates on their performance, the neo-literates are categorised occupation-wise into two groups i.e., agriculture labour and agriculture and others and their respective mean performance scores are calculated and 't' test is applied to find out the significant difference if any between the two occupation groups. The results show that the agriculture and others have obtained better performance scores than the agriculture labour. In addition, the calculated 't' test shows that the difference between the mean performance of the two groups of neo-literates is found to be significant at 0.01 level.

(f) Performance V/s Income

Based on the level of income, the neo-literates are categorised into two groups viz., less income (less than Rs. 10,000 income per annum) and more income (more than Rs. 10,000 income per annum) and their performance scores are calculated and presented in the Table 5.20. The trend of the obtained mean performance scores of the neo-literates with less income and more income shows that the neo-literates with more income are found to be better in their performance than the low income group. However, the calculated 't' value is not significant.

(g) Performance V/s Type of Family

The results presented in the Table 5.20 clearly shows that the influence of the type of family viz., nuclear and joint families on the neo-literates performance. The trend of the mean performance scores obtained by the two groups of neo-literates i.e., nuclear and joint families clearly shows that the neo-literates from joint families have shown better performance than the nuclear family. However, the obtained 't' value is not significant. It shows that the type of family is not a significant predictor of the neo-literate performance.

(h) Performance V/s Number of Children

In order to find out the influence of the number of children possessed by the neo-literates on their performance, the neo-literates are categorised into three groups based on the children viz., no child, one child and two and more children. The trend of the mean performance scores are calculated and 'F' value is applied to find out the significant difference if any amongst the three groups. The results presented in the Table 5.20 show that the neo-literates having no children are found to be better performers than the other two groups. But, the results of the 'F' value indicates that there is no significant difference between the above three groups of neo-literates.

In view of the above findings, the hypothesis "there is no significant influence of the socio-economic and demographic characteristics on the performance of the neo-literates" is accepted in case of the marital status, caste, income, type of family and number of children and the hypothesis is not accepted in the case of sex, age and occupation.

SUMMING UP

From the above analysis, it is clear that the performance of the neo-literates is significantly influenced by the variables such as sex, age and occupation. The analysis also illustrates that men, unmarried, 35 years and above, backward caste, agriculture and others, more income, joint family and no children are found to be better performers than others. Steps should be taken to improve the performance of low scoring groups of neo-literates.

Table 5.21: Means, SDs and t/F value for the Performance of Neo-literates

Sl. No.	*Level of Performance*	*N*	*Mean*	*S.D.*	*t/F*
1.	High level	114	71.54	6.27	
	Medium level	126	67.61	9.86	21.53**
	Low level	120	64.05	9.31	
2.	High level	114	71.54	6.27	3.71**
	Medium level	126	67.61	9.86	
3.	High level	114	71.54	6.27	7.24**
	Low level	120	64.05	9.31	
4.	Medium level	114	67.61	9.86	3.09**
	Low level	120	64.05	9.31	

** Significant at 0.01 level

It is assumed that, the performance of the preraks is likely to influence the performance of neo-literates as well.

In the present study, an attempt is made to know whether the neo-literates performance (neo-literates performance with regard to 3R's i.e., reading, writing and arithmetic) is influenced by the performance of preraks. As a first step, the preraks are divided into three groups (high, medium and low) based upon the criteria of mean ±1/2 standard deviation. The respective scores of neo-literates studying under the preraks are considered. As per this criteria, out of 360 neo-literates, 114 (32 per cent) fall under the category of high level performance, 126 (35 per cent) fall under medium level performance and remaining 120 (33 per cent) are in the category of low level performance. 'F' test is employed to see whether, there exists any significant difference in the mean performance of the neo-literates in 3R's studying under the preraks. The 'F' value shows that the difference among the three groups of neo-literates is found to be statistically significant at 0.01 level.

High level V/s Medium level Performance

In order to study the impact of literacy of neo-literates on their performance, the neo-literates are categorised into two groups viz., high and medium level and their respective mean performance scores are calculated and 't' test is applied to find out the difference if any between the two groups. The results presented in the Table 5.21 indicates that high level performance group has obtained better performance scores than the medium level performance group. Further, it also shows that the difference between the mean performance scores of the neo-literates with high, medium level group is significant at 0.01 level.

High level V/s Low level Performance

In order to bring out the influence of literacy of the neo-literates on their level of performance, the neo-literates are categorised into two groups viz., high and low level and their respective mean performance scores are calculated and 't' test is applied to find out the significant difference if any between the two groups. The results presented in the Table 5.21 illustrates that high level performance group has obtained better performance scores than the low level performance group. In addition, the 't' test result shows that the difference between mean performance is significant at 0.01 level.

Medium level V/s Low level Performance

In order to study the influence of literacy of the neo-literates on their level of performance, the neo-literates are categorised into two groups viz., medium and low level. The trend of the mean performance scores of the neo-literates show that medium level performers have obtained better scores than low level performance group. Further, the 't' test also states that neo-literates are found to be significant. Hence, the hypothesis "preraks performance does not significantly influence the performance of neo-literates" is not accepted. Hence, appropriate measures should be taken by the Zilla Saksharatha Samithi, such as effective prerak teaching, special literacy classes, special concentration on drop-outs, personal motivation, personal care and interest to improve the standards of low level performers.

CLASSIFICATION OF THE PROBLEMS OF THE NEO-LITERATES

In order to identify the problems of the neo-literates in attending the continuing education centres, a 5-point rating scale was administered to them. In order to categorise the problems, the method of mean ±1/2 standard deviation was followed. The problems of the neo-literates are categorised as more prominent, prominent and less prominent. The items having 907.71 and less mean values are taken as less prominent problems, the mean values between 907.72 to 1011.28 are taken as prominent problems and the items mean 1011.29 and above are rated as more prominent problems. As per this categorisation, out of the 34 problems, 11 items are found to be more prominent problems, 14 items are found to be prominent problems and 10 items as less prominent problems. 40 per cent of the problems are found to be prominent problems among the neo-literates in attending the continuing education centres. The detailed discussion on the three categories of the problems of the neo-literates is presented below.

(a) More Prominent Problems

The first category of the problems i.e., more prominent problems of the neo-literates identified are as follows:

Table 5.22: More Prominent Problems and their respective Mean values checked by the Neo-literates

Sl. No.	*More Prominent Problems*	*Mean Value*
1.	Financial problems.	1197.00
2.	Self-employment opportunities are not provided.	1127.00
3.	Centre is not organised properly.	1118.00
4.	Women neo-literates feel shy to attend the centre.	1092.00
5.	Inefficiency of teaching.	1086.00
6.	Heavy work at home.	1065.00
7.	Lack of books in continuing education centre.	1040.00
8.	Difficulty in dealing with reading, writing and arithmetic.	1034.00
9.	Child rearing.	1033.00
10.	Library and reading room is not available.	1022.00
11.	Dailies, weeklies, fortnightly and monthly magazines are not supplied.	1019.00

From the Table 5.22, it becomes clear that, out of 34 problems, 11 items are found to be more prominent problems of the neo-literates. The neo-literate problems are further categorised into two types viz., personal problems and programme related problems. Out of 11 problems, 6 items come under programme related problems viz., centre is not organised properly, inefficiency of teaching, lack of books in continuing education centre, non-availability of library and reading room, dailies, weeklies, fortnightly and monthly magazines, lack of self-employment opportunities. Personal problems of the preraks are financial problems, heavy work, difficulty in dealing with reading, writing and arithmetic, shyness of women neo-literates in attending the continuing education centres and child rearing duties of the women.

(b) Prominent Problems

The second category of the problems i.e., prominent problems of the preraks identified are as follows:

Table 5.23: Prominent Problems and their respective Mean values checked by the Neo-literates

Sl. No.	*Prominent Problems*	*Mean Value*
1.	Centre is far away.	1005.00
2.	Quality of life improvement programmes are not organised.	992.00
3.	Family problems.	989.00
4.	Lack of even minimum facilities.	980.00
5.	Primers are difficult to learn.	961.00
6.	Agriculture work.	950.00
7.	Inadequate space at the centre.	944.00
8.	Non co-operation of the preraks.	941.00
9.	Lack of unity among the neo-literates due to political conflicts.	935.00
10.	Inconvenient timings of the centre.	929.00
11.	Lack of awareness among neo-literates about continuing education.	922.00
12.	No separate centres for women.	922.00
13.	Lack of interest on education.	920.00
14.	Lack of time to attend the centres.	917.00

From Table 5.23, it appears that out of 34 problems, 14 items are found to be prominent problems of the neo-literates. Out of 14 problems, 8 items are programme related problems, remaining 6 problems are personal problems. Programme related problems of the neo-literates are centre is located far away, lack of minimum facilities, inadequate space at the centre, inconvenient timings, lack of awareness among neo-literates about continuing education, primers are difficult to learn, no separate centres for women and lack of quality of life improvement programmes. Organisational problems are predominant and appropriate measures should be taken to solve these organisational problems.

Neo-literate personal problems are family problems, lack of interest on education, lack of time to attend the continuing education centre, lack of unity among the neo-literates, non co-operation of the preraks, participation in agriculture work.

Less Prominent Problems

The third category of the problems i.e., less prominent problems of the neo-literates are as follows:

Table 5.24: Less Prominent Problems and their respective Mean values checked by the Neo-literates

Sl. No.	*Less Prominent Problems*	*Mean Value*
1.	Bad habits.	893.00
2.	Lack of co-operation from the villagers and village leaders.	876.00
3.	Poor health.	866.00
4.	Primers are not related to their real life.	864.00
5.	Lack of co-operation from the family members.	860.00
6.	Migration to other places in search work.	835.00
7.	No discussion and debate programmes at the centre.	795.00
8.	Equivalency programmes are not organised at the centre.	767.00
9.	Individual interest promotion programmes are not organised at the centre.	727.00

The Table 5.24 indicates that the problems of the neo-literates in participating the continuing education centres. Out of the 34 problems, 9 items are found to be less prominent problems of the neo-literates. One fourth of the problems are less prominent problems. The problems are divided into two groups i.e., personal and programmes related problems. Out of the 9 problems, 5 items fall under personal problems viz., bad habits, poor health, migration to other places in search work, lack of co-operation from the family members, villagers and village leaders. The programme related problems are primers are not related to their real life, no discussion and debate programmes at the centre, equivalency programmes and individual interest promotion programmes are not organised at the centre.

Table 5.25: Mean problem score, SDs obtained by the Neo-literates of three groups and 'F' value

S. No.	*Groups*	*N*	*Mean*	*SD*	*F*
1.	More prominent problems	105	101.46	5.85	
2.	Prominent problems	145	90.49	2.75	649.97**
3.	Less prominent problems	110	80.42	4.08	

** Significant at 0.01 level

40 per cent of the neo-literates are facing moderate problems in attending the continuing education centre activities. 29 per cent of the neo-literates are found to be facing more problems to attend the continuing education centres. In other words, this high risk group if not tackled properly, may lead to failure of the continuing education centre activities in all fronts. Hence, appropriate measures should be taken to rectify the problems by conducting the short term training programmes to this group of neo-literates to overcome the problems at the initial stage itself. The above results clearly indicate that the intensity of problems faced by the neo-literates is not similar and each group feels it differently. Further, the calculated 'F' value shows that they are significant at 0.01 level among the three groups of neo-literates in terms of their mean problem scores. Hence, the hypothesis "the intensity of the problems encountered by the neo-literates in attending the continuing education centres is not similar" is accepted.

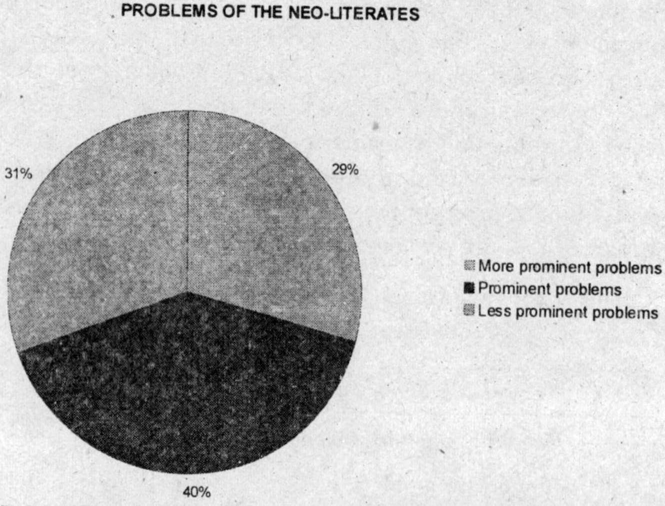

Table 5.26: Problem Areas and respective Mean problems scores, SDs and 't' Test

Sl. No.	*Problem Area*	*N*	*Mean*	*SD*	*'t'*
1.	Personal problems	120	42.78	5.77	11.47**
2.	Programme related problems	120	47.83	6.03	

** Significant at 0.01 level

The trend of the mean problem scores shows that the neo-literates personal problems are found to be facing fewer problems than the programme related problems. Further, the calculated 't' value also shows that the difference between these two areas is significant at 0.01 level. Hence, the hypothesis "there is no significant difference between the neo-literates personal problems and programme related problems" is not accepted.

In order to find out the association between the socio-economic and demographic characteristics and personal problem of the neo-literates, they are classified into different groups based on their characteristics and problems. The chi-square test is applied and the findings are presented in the Table 5.27. Association between socio-economic and demographic characteristics and the personal problems shows

Table 5.27: Distribution of Chi-square values in respect of the Socio-economic and Demographic Characteristics of the Neo-literates in the problem area of Personal Problems

Sl. No.	*Variable*	*D.F.*	χ^2
1.	Sex	2	1.83@
2.	Marital Status	2	0.05@
3.	Age	4	6.76@
4.	Caste	4	12.64*
5.	Occupation	2	4.35@
6.	Income	2	7.60*
7.	Type of Family	2	0.90@
8.	Number of Children	4	1.70@

@ Not significant* Significant at 0.05 level

that the association is significant in the case of caste and income. Hence, the hypothesis "there is no significant association between the socio-economic and demographic characteristics and personal problems encountered by the neo-literates in attending the continuing education centres" is not accepted in the case of caste and income. However, the association is not significant in the case of sex, marital status, age, occupation, type of family and number of children, hence, the hypothesis is accepted with regard to all the above mentioned variables.

The results presented in the Table 5.28 shows that there is no significant difference between different groups of neo-literates belonging to different characteristics except in the case of income. Hence, the hypothesis "there is no significant relationship between the socio-economic and demographic characteristics and the personal problems encountered by the neo-literates in attending the continuing education centres" is accepted except in the case of income. The trend of the mean problem score demonstrates that men neo-literates,

Table 5.28: Mean problem scores, SDs obtained by the Neo-literates belonging to different groups along with t/F values in the area of Personal Problems

Sl. No.	*Variable*	*Groups*	*N*	*Mean*	*S.D.*	*t/F*
1.	Sex	Men	180	42.55	5.90	0.75@
		Women	180	43.01	5.62	
2.	Marital Status	Married	257	42.91	5.82	0.65@
		Unmarried	103	42.47	5.62	
3.	Age	15-24	149	42.71	5.48	
		25-34	136	42.70	6.22	0.11@
		35+	75	43.06	5.44	
4.	Caste	SC/ST	148	42.30	6.06	
		BC	114	42.82	5.74	1.20@
		OC	98	43.46	5.25	
5.	Occupation	Agriculture labour	255	42.57	5.78	1.10@
		Agriculture and others	105	43.30	5.69	
6.	Income	< 10,000 (Less)	221	42.25	5.90	2.24*
		10,001-20,000/- (More)	139	43.62	5.44	
7.	Type of Family	Nuclear	271	42.84	5.77	0.36@
		Joint	89	42.59	5.74	
8.	Number of children	No child	119	42.35	5.46	
		One	131	43.03	6.34	0.50@
		2 and above	110	42.96	5.33	

@ Not Significant *Significant at 0.05 level

unmarried, 25-34 years age group, SC/ST, agriculture labour, less income, joint family and no children are found to be facing fewer problems in the personal sphere.

The results presented in the Table 5.29 indicates that, there is no significant association between neo-literate programme related problems and socio-economic and demographic characteristics of the neo-literates viz., sex, marital status, age, caste, occupation, income, type of family and number of children. Hence, the hypothesis "there is no

Table 5.29: Distribution of Chi-square values in respect of the Socio-economic and Demographic Characteristics of the Neo-literates in the problem area of Programme related Problems

Sl. No.	*Variable*	*D.F.*	χ^2
1.	Sex	2	0.42@
2.	Marital Status	2	1.29@
3.	Age	4	0.50@
4.	Caste	4	2.22@
5.	Occupation	2	5.84@
6.	Income	2	4.63@
7.	Type of Family	2	2.06@
8.	Number of Children	4	2.09@

@ Not significant

significant association between the socio-economic and demographic characteristics and the programme related problems encountered by the neo-literates in attending the continuing education centres" is accepted in case of the above variables.

The Table 5.30 shows that the results relating to the relationship between socio-economic and demographic characteristics and problems of the neo-literates in the area of programme related problems. The calculated t/F values shows that there is no significant difference between mean problem scores of the neo-literates belonging to sex, marital status, age, caste, occupation, income, type of family and number of children. Hence, the hypothesis "there is no significant relationship between the socio-economic and demographic characteristics and the programme related problems encountered by the neo-literates in attending the continuing education centres" is accepted. The trend of the mean problem score indicates that the neo-literates belonging to women, unmarried, 15-24 years age group, O.C.,

Table 5.30: Mean problem scores, SDs obtained by the Neo-literates belonging to different groups along with t/F values in the area of Programme related Problems

Sl. No.	*Variable*	*Groups*	*N*	*Mean*	*S.D.*	*t/F*
1.	Sex	Men	180	48.00	5.89	0.52@
		Women	180	47.66	6.16	
2.	Marital Status	Married	257	47.87	5.90	0.18@
		Unmarried	103	47.73	6.35	
3.	Age	15-24	149	47.31	6.12	
		25-34	136	48.22	5.85	0.93@
		35+	75	48.14	6.11	
4.	Caste	SC/ST	148	47.71	6.39	
		BC	114	48.34	6.00	0.66@
		OC	98	47.41	5.44	
5.	Occupation	Agriculture labour	255	47.98	6.31	0.81@
		Agriculture and others	105	47.45	5.27	
6.	Income	< 10,000 (Less)	221	47.79	6.53	0.17@
		10,001-20,000/- (More)	139	47.89	5.13	
7.	Type of Family	Nuclear	271	47.95	6.19	0.71@
		Joint	89	47.46	5.49	
8.	Number of children	No child	119	47.58	6.31	
		One	131	48.60	6.29	1.80@
		2 and above	110	47.18	5.25	

@ Not Significant

agriculture, less income, joint family and two and more children faced fewer problems than the other groups.

The neo-literates are classified into different groups based on their socio-economic and demographic characteristics and problems. The chi-square test is applied and the findings presented in the Table 5.31. The association between socio-economic and demographic characteristics and the problems of neo-literates shows that the association is not significant in case of sex, marital status, age, caste, occupation, income, type of family and number of children. Hence, the hypothesis

Table 5.31: Distribution of Chi-square values in respect of the Socio-economic and Demographic Characteristics of the Neo-literates in the Problems (Total)

Sl. No.	*Variable*	*D.F.*	χ^2
1.	Sex	2	5.10@
2.	Marital Status	2	0.40@
3.	Age	4	1.49@
4.	Caste	4	4.42@
5.	Occupation	2	0.16@
6.	Income	2	3.96@
7.	Type of Family	2	0.51@
8.	Number of Children	4	5.88@

@ Not significant

"there is no significant association between socio-economic and demographic characteristics and problems encountered by the neo-literates in attending the continuing education centres" is accepted.

Table 5.32: Mean problem scores, SDs obtained by the Neo-literates belonging to different groups along with t/F values in the Total Problems

S. No.	*Variable*	*Groups*	*N*	*Mean*	*S.D.*	*t/F*
1	*2*	*3*	*4*	*5*	*6*	*7*
1.	Sex	Men	180	90.55	9.11	0.13@
		Women	180	90.68	9.23	
2.	Marital Status	Married	257	90.78	9.32	0.54@
		Unmarried	103	90.21	8.77	
3.	Age	15-24	149	90.03	8.61	
		25-34	136	90.93	9.46	0.53@
		35+	75	91.21	9.65	

(contd.)

1	2	3	4	5	6	7
4.	Caste	SC/ST	148	90.02	9.59	
		BC	114	91.16	8.84	0.55@
		OC	98	90.88	8.84	
5.	Occupation	Agriculture labour	255	90.56	9.27	0.19@
		Agriculture and others	105	90.76	8.92	
6.	Income	< 10,000 (Less)	221	90.05	9.56	1.53@
		10,001-20,000/- (More)	139	91.52	8.45	
7.	Type of Family	Nuclear	271	90.80	9.20	0.67@
		Joint	89	90.05	9.05	
8.	Number of children	No child	119	89.94	8.82	
		One	131	91.63	10.37	1.26@
		2 and above	110	90.14	7.81	

@ Not Significant

(a) Problems V/s Sex

The aim of the programme is to provide literacy to the all sections of the community. As a result of this, both sex groups participated in continuing education centre activities. The mean problem scores of the two groups are calculated and 't' test is applied to study the differences if any between these two groups. The calculated mean problems score of men and women indicates that men neo-literates found to be facing fewer problems than the women neo-literates. The 't' value indicates that the difference is not significant.

(b) Problems V/s Marital Status

The sample neo-literates are categorised into two groups viz., married and unmarried, their respective mean problem scores are calculated to understand the influence of marital status on problems facing in attending continuing education centres. The trend of the mean problem scores are presented in the Table 5.32 and shows that unmarried neo-literates are found to be facing lesser problems than the married neo-literates. Further, the calculated 't' value also indicates that the differences between the mean problem scores of the married and unmarried neo-literates is not significant.

INFLUENCE OF THE SOCIO-ECONOMIC AND DEMOGRAPHIC CHARACTERISTICS ON THE PROBLEMS OF THE NEO-LITERATES

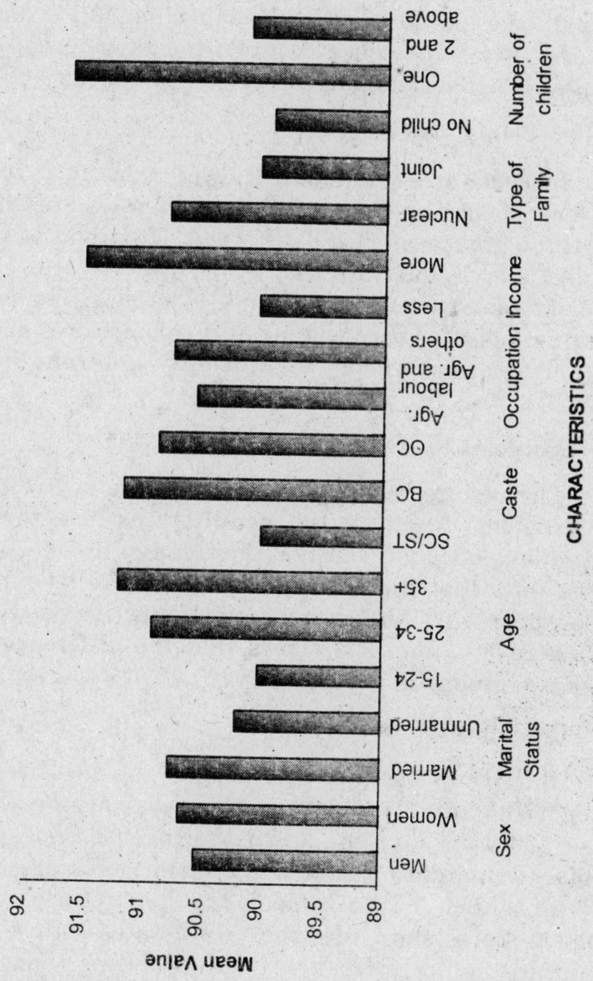

(c) Problems V/s Age

In order to study the influence of age of neo-literates on their problems, the neo-literates are categorised into three age groups viz., 15-24, 25-34 and 35 years and above and their respective mean problem scores demonstrates that the neo-literates of 15-24 years age group are found to be facing fewer problems than the other two groups i.e., 25-34 years age and 35 years age and above. On the other hand, 'F' value shows that the mean difference between the three groups of neo-literates is not significant.

(d) Problems V/s Caste

In order to understand the influence of caste on the problems of the neo-literates, the neo-literates are categorised into three groups as SC/ST, BC, OC. The trend of the mean problem scores illustrate that SC/ST neo-literates are facing lesser problems than the OC and BC groups. The calculated 'F' value indicates that the mean problem scores of all these three categories are not significantly different from each other.

(e) Problems V/s Occupation

The results relating to the influence of occupation on the problems faced by the neo-literates in attending the continuing education centres, the trend of the mean problem scores show that the neo-literate agriculture labourers faced fewer problems than the agriculture and others. The calculated 't' value also shows that the difference between these two groups is not significant.

(f) Problems V/s Income

Based on the level of income, the neo-literates are categorised into two groups i.e., less income (less than Rs. 10,000 per annum) and more income (more than Rs. 10,000 per annum) and their problem scores are calculated and presented in the table 5.32. The trend of the mean problem scores show that the neo-literates with less income group are found to be facing less problems than the more income group. The 't' value indicates that difference between these two groups is not significant.

(g) Problems V/s Type of Family

The results presented in the Table 5.32 clearly shows that the influence of the type of family viz., nuclear and joint families, on the problems of neo-literates. The trend of the mean problem scores obtained by the two groups of neo-literates viz., nuclear and joint families clearly indicate that the neo-literates from joint families faced fewer problems than the neo-literates belonging to nuclear families. However, the obtained 't' value is not significant.

(h) Problems V/s Number of Children

For analysing the influence of the children on the problems faced by the neo-literates in attending the continuing education centres, neo-literates are classified into three groups viz., neo-literates with no children, one child and two and more children. The problem scores of the neo-literates of the three groups illustrate that the neo-literates with no children are found to be facing fewer problems followed by neo-literates with two and more children and one child.

The Table 5.32 illustrates that there is no significant relationship between the mean problem scores of the neo-literates and their socio-economic and demographic characteristics. Hence, the hypothesis "there is no significant relationship between the socio-economic and demographic characteristics and the problems encountered by the neo-literates in attending the continuing education centres" is accepted in case of all the variables.

SUMMING UP

From the above analysis, it is clear that, the neo-literates belonging to men, unmarried, 15-24 years age group, SC/ST, agriculture labour, less income, joint family and no child are found to be facing fewer problems in attending the continuing education centres. Women neo-literates, married, 25-34 years age group, BC, agriculture and others, more income, nuclear family and one child are found to be facing more number of problems.

COMMUNITY OPINION ON THE PERFORMANCE OF PRERAKS

In the present study an attempt is made to know the positive and negative opinions of the representatives of the community towards continuing education. The attitude score obtained by the community representatives are categorised into two groups based upon mean ±1/2 standard deviation. The items on which the community representatives have obtained scores equivalent and above mean +1/2 standard deviation are treated as those possessing high positive opinion and the scores equivalent and below the range of mean -1/2 standard deviation are treated as those representing negative opinion. Out of 45 items on 19 items, the opinion is positive and on 26 items the opinion is negative.

Positive Opinion of Community Representatives

Table 5.33 give the items on which positive opinion is expressed by the community.

It is evident from the Table 5.33, the community feels that, the preraks are good with regard to the aspect such as creation of awareness about DWCRA, CMEY, TRYSEM and Deepam, organising literacy awareness programmes through kalajathas, street plays, dances, slogans and folk arts, discussion about individual development of the neo-literates, social evils and dowry. Further, community opinion is positive on the organisation of programmes related to literacy and development, organising discussion groups on safe drinking water, health, diseases and traffic rules, conducting short-term training programmes like leadership qualities, right to vote, agriculture, animal husbandry, embroidery and tailoring, organising cycle rallies in the village, facilitating the neo-literates participation in group discussion, improving the literacy skills in the evening classes of neo-literates, helping self-help groups to acquire literacy, organising activities related to individual members, singing competitions and vocational training programmes. Community opinion is also favourable in the following functions of the preraks like, taking steps to maintain the records and reports such as forwarding different types of reports to Nodal Prerak,

Table 5.33: Positive Opinion and their respective Mean values checked by the Community Representatives

S. No.	*Positive Opinion*	*Mean Value*
1.	Creating awareness about DWCRA, CMEY, TRYSEM and Deepam.	1230.00
2.	Organisation of discussion groups (drinking water, health, diseases and traffic rules)	1182.00
3.	Organising cycle rallies in the village.	1182.00
4.	Organising short-term training programmes (leadership, qualities, right to vote, agriculture, embroidery and tailoring).	1126.00
5.	Organising literacy awareness through kalajathas, street plays, dances and slogans.	1100.00
6.	Forwarding different types of reports to Nodal Prerak.	1052.00
7.	Facilitating neo-literates participation in group discussion.	1036.00
8.	Recording information about the village.	1018.00
9.	Maintaining records and registers in the centre.	1008.00
10.	Organising vocational training programmes.	1000.00
11.	Improving literacy skills of neo-literates in the evening classes.	992.00
12.	Collection of corpus fund through village education committees.	990.00
13.	Helping self-help groups to acquire literacy.	986.00
14.	Organising activities related to development as per the desire of the individuals.	946.00
15.	Organising singing competitions.	922.00
16.	Creating awareness on folk arts.	912.00
17.	Discussion about individual development of the neo-literates.	910.00
18.	Discussion on social evils and dowry.	902.00
19.	Participation in the review meetings and training programmes.	894.00

recording information about village and maintaining records and registers in the centre. Preraks participation in the review meetings and training programmes and collection of corpus fund through village education committees.

Negative Opinion of the Community Representatives

Out of 45 items, on 26 items, the community has negative opinion as shown in table 5.3.

Table 5.34: Negative Opinion and their respective Mean values checked by the Community Representatives

Sl. No.	*Negative Opinion*	*Mean Value*
1	*2*	*3*
1.	Organising equivalency programmes.	888.00
2.	Providing minimum facilities to the neo-literates.	886.00
3.	Arranging cultural programmes with the help of local cultural troops.	880.00
4.	Organising quality of life improvement programmes.	872.00
5.	Supplying daily newspapers, monthly and fortnight magazines to the centre.	866.00
6.	Discussion about the individual and village issues.	856.00
7.	Identification the learning needs of the neo-literates and preparing a plan to meet these needs.	854.00
8.	Motivating the neo-literates to participate in games and sports.	840.00
9.	Creating conducive educational environment in the centre.	826.00
10.	Collecting the information about development programmes.	814.00
11.	Discussion about the population, family planning and pollution.	810.00
12.	Collection of the funds and books to organise the library.	800.00

1	2	3
13.	Organising self-employment programmes.	794.00
14.	Keeping records in continuing education centres about literacy and illiteracy in the village.	794.00
15.	Organising recreational activities.	784.00
16.	Running the centre for six days in a week.	780.00
17.	Organising continuing education centre programmes through the village education committees.	778.00
18.	Teaching the importance of games and sports to neo-literates.	764.00
19.	Running the library and reading room.	762.00
20.	Conducting sports and games competitions.	742.00
21.	Running the information centre.	740.00
22.	Getting help from Mandal Literacy Organisers and supervisors in organising the continuing education centre activities.	734.00
23.	Collection of books related to social, scientific, art and history.	712.00
24.	Evaluating the progress of the centres.	696.00
25.	Arranging audio-visual aids.	690.00
26.	Making aware of the uses of the games and sports.	676.00

The community representatives feel that, the performance of preraks is poor in issues related to provision of minimum facilities in the centre, supply of daily newspapers, weekly, monthly magazines, collection of books related to social, scientific, art and history and in arranging the audio-visual aids. The communities opinion is also poor on the activities like organising equivalency programmes, quality life improvement programmes, self-employment programmes, continuing education centre programmes through village education committees, arranging cultural programmes with the help of local cultural troops and recreational activities, discussion about the individual and village issues, population, pollution, family planning and national values, identifying the learning needs of the neo-literates and preparing a plan to meet these needs, collection of information about development programmes, keeping the records in continuing education centres about literacy and illiteracy in the village, running the library and reading room in the centre, conducting the sports and games competitions, running the information centre and evaluating the progress of the centres, collection of finances to organise the library.

Table 5.35: Means, SDs and 't' test for the Community Opinion of Community Representatives

Sl. No.	*Community Opinion*	*N*	*Mean*	*SD*	*'t'*
1.	Positive	160	120.83	7.96	22.64**
2.	Negative	200	103.46	6.20	

** Significant at 0.01 level

The Table 5.35 clearly shows that 44 (160) per cent of the community representatives opined that the preraks performance was good in all aspects of continuing education centres. On the other hand, 56 (200) per cent of the community representatives have negative opinion about the capacity of the preraks. Based on the opinion, the community representatives are categorised into two groups viz., positive and negative attitude members and their attitude scores are calculated and presented in the Table 5.35. The trend of the obtained mean scores of the community representatives and difference between the positive and negative groups and 't' test is found that there is significant difference at 0.01 level. The second group of community representatives expressed poor opinion against the preraks. Hence, the hypothesis "there is no significant difference between the positive and negative opinions on the performance of preraks" is not accepted.

RELATIONSHIP BETWEEN PRERAKS PERFORMANCE/ PROBLEMS AND NEO-LITERATES PERFORMANCE/PROBLEMS

In order to understand the relationship between performance and problems of the preraks and neo-literates. In order to study the preraks/neo-literates are categorised into two groups based on their mean scores. The tables 5.36 shows that the mean scores, S.Ds obtained by the preraks/neo-literates and their respective 't' values.

Table 5.36: Mean performance scores, SDs obtained by the Preraks and Neo-literates along with 't' Test in the area of Performance

Sl. No.	*Performance*	*N*	*Mean*	*SD*	*'t'*
1.	Preraks performance	120	126.80	8.23	66.10**
2.	Neo-literates performance	360	67.67	9.19	

** Significant at 0.01 level

Preraks Performance V/s Neo-literates

In order to measure the performance of two groups viz., preraks and neo-literates and their respective mean performance scores are calculated. The trend of the mean performance scores shows that the preraks have obtained better performance than the neo-literates performance. In addition, the 't' test result shows that the difference between the preraks and neo-literates performance is significant at 0.01 level. Hence, the hypothesis "there is no significant difference between the preraks performance and neo-literates performance" is not accepted. Hence, the preraks performed their specific functions properly viz., organisation of evening classes, maintaining the library and reading room, conducting training programmes of short duration, organising charcha mandal, conducting sports and games, recreational and cultural activities, and acted as a information window and communication centre.

Table 5.37: Mean problem scores, SDs obtained by the Preraks and Neo-literates along with 't' Test in the area of Problems

S. No.	*Problems*	*N*	*Mean*	*SD*	*'t'*
1.	Preraks problems	120	105.36	8.08	16.71**
2.	Neo-literates problems	360	90.61	9.17	

** Significant at 0.01 level

Preraks Problems V/s Neo-literates

The trend of the mean problem scores illustrates that the neo-literates are facing fewer problems than the preraks and 't' test is applied to find out the difference between these two groups and it is significant at 0.01 level. Hence, the hypothesis "there is no significant difference between the prerak problems and neo-literates problems" is not accepted. Preraks are facing innumeral problems of personal and programme related, while the neo-literates are facing less problems than the preraks.

Table 5.38: Mean scores, SDs obtained by the Preraks Performance and Community Opinion along with 't' Test

S. No.	*Groups*	*N*	*Mean*	*SD*	*'t'*
1.	Preraks performance	120	128.51	8.26	18.12**
2.	Community representatives opinion	360	111.18	11.14	

** Significant at 0.01 level

Preraks Performance V/s Community Representatives Opinion

In order to measure the preraks performance and community representatives opinions and their respective mean scores are calculated. The trend of the mean scores shows that the preraks have obtained better performance scores than the community representatives. In addition, the 't' test result shows that the difference between the preraks and community representatives opinion is significant at 0.01 level. Hence, the hypothesis "there is no significant difference between the preraks performance and community representatives opinion" is not accepted.

6

SUMMARY AND CONCLUSIONS

Literacy is one of the key element of human resource development. In order to improve the quality of human resources of the country, the Government of India has launched a number of adult education programmes for the promotion of literacy. As a result, a large pool of newly made literates were created. In order to prevent them to relapse into illiteracy and institutionalise continuing education programme, the scheme of continuing education centres were launched through out the country.

Major objectives of continuing education is to provide facilities for retention, continuing education and application of functional literacy, dissemination of information, creation of awareness about national concerns, improvement of economic condition, improved productivity, recreation and healthy living etc. Each continuing education centre is headed by a prerak and is expected to serve around 500 neo-literates in a population about 1500 to 2000. In order to achieve the above, the continuing education centres have to perform specific functions viz., organisation of evening classes, maintaining library and a reading room, conducting training programmes of short duration, organising charcha Mandal (group discussion), conduct sports and games, recreational and cultural activities and act as a information window and communication centre.

In view of the above, the continuing education centres should perform a number of functions not only for retention of literacy but also to accelerate the socio-economic development of the country. Hence, it is necessary to have the knowledge of the activities that are being undertaken inside the continuing education centre and in the community. This will go a long way in formulating effective strategies for improving quality of the programme and to modify the various aspects suitable to the local conditions. The efficiency of the continuing education centre lies on the effective performance of various roles by the prerak. In view of this, the present study is formulated to study the functioning of continuing education centres in Nellore District of Andhra Pradesh.

OBJECTIVES

The specific objectives of the study are as follows:

Principal Objective

- To study the performance of the continuing education centres with special reference to preraks and neo-literates.

Subsidiary Objectives

- To identify the problems of the continuing education centres with special reference to preraks and neo-literates.
- To study the relationship amongst performance, problems and socio-economic and demographic characteristics of the preraks.
- To study the relationship amongst performance, problems and socio-economic and demographic characteristics of the neo-literates.
- To assess the community opinion towards the functioning of continuing education centres.

HYPOTHESES

On the basis of the above objectives, the following hypotheses are formulated for testing.

- The level of performance of the preraks working in continuing education centres is not similar.
- There is no significant association between the socio-economic and demographic characteristics

and performance of the preraks working in continuing education centres.

- There is no significant relationship between the socio-economic and demographic characteristics and performance of the preraks working in continuing education centres.
- The intensity of the problems encountered by the preraks, working in continuing education centres is not similar.
- There is no significant difference between the prerak personal problems and programme related problems.
- There is no significant association between the socio-economic and demographic characteristics and the personal problems encountered by the preraks in organising the continuing education centres.
- There is no significant relationship between the socio-economic and demographic characteristics and the personal problems encountered by the preraks in organising the continuing education centres.
- There is no significant association between the socio-economic and demographic characteristics and the programme related problems encountered by the preraks in organising the continuing education centres.
- There is no significant relationship between the socio-economic and demographic characteristics and the programme related problems encountered by the preraks in organising the continuing education centres.
- There is no significant association between socio-economic and demographic characteristics and the problems encountered by the preraks in organising the continuing education centres.

- There is no significant relationship between socio-economic and demographic characteristics and the problems encountered by the preraks in organising the continuing education centres.
- The level of the performance of the neo-literates attending the continuing education centres is not similar.
- There is no significant association between the socio-economic and demographic characteristics and performance of the neo-literates.
- There is no significant influence of the socio-economic and demographic characteristics on the performance of the neo-literates.
- Preraks performance does not significantly influence the performance of neo-literates.
- The intensity of the problems encountered by the neo-literates in attending continuing education centres is not similar.
- There is no significant difference between the neo-literates personal problems and programme related problems.
- There is no significant association between the socio-economic and demographic characteristics and personal problems encountered by the neo-literates in attending the continuing education centres.
- There is no significant relationship between the socio-economic and demographic characteristics and the personal problems encountered by the neo-literates in attending the continuing education centres.
- There is no significant association between the socio-economic and demographic characteristics and the programme related problems encountered by the neo-literates in attending the continuing education centres.

- There is no significant relationship between the socio-economic and demographic characteristics and the programme related problems encountered by the neo-literates.
- There is no significant association between socio-economic and demographic characteristics and problems encountered by the neo-literates in attending the continuing education centres.
- There is no significant relationship between the socio-economic and demographic characteristics and problems encountered by the neo-literates in attending the continuing education centres.
- There is no significant difference between positive and negative opinions of the performance of preraks.
- There is no significant difference between the preraks performance and neo-literates performance.
- There is no significant difference between the preraks problems and neo-literates problems.
- There is no significant difference between the preraks performance and community representatives opinion.

Variables Studied

Three variables viz., performance of the preraks and neo-literates and problems of the preraks and neo-literates and community opinion on the performance of preraks are considered as dependent variables of the study. The socio-economic and demographic characteristics of the preraks and neo-literates viz., sex, marital status, age, caste, education, occupation, experience, income, type of family and number of children are chosen as independent variables of the study.

Tools

For testing the above hypothesis, certain data have to be collected form different sources. Hence, the investigator

has developed the tools viz., preraks performance, preraks problem inventory, achievement test in literacy for neo-literates, neo-literates problem inventory and community opinion on the performance of preraks.

Sample

The locale of the study is continuing education centres in the Nellore District of Andhra Pradesh. The universe of the study constitutes 356 continuing education centres functioning in the district under the supervision of Zilla Saksharatha Samithi. For the purpose of present study 120 (CECs) preraks were chosen at random. 360 neo-literates and 360 community representatives from the villages with continuing education centres were selected randomly. Thus, the sample of the study constitutes 120 preraks, 360 neo-literates and 360 community representatives.

The data were collected from the selected sample by administering the relevant tools. The data thus collected were pooled together and analysed by using suitable statistical techniques like mean, S.D., 't' test, chi-square test and ANOVA.

MAJOR FINDINGS

The major findings of the study are as follows:

- Based on the preraks performance out of 120 continuing education centres, 38 continuing education centres performance are of high level, 42 continuing education centres performance is of medium level and remaining 40 continuing education centres have performed at low level.
- The level of the performance of the preraks working in continuing education centres differs from group to group.
- The high level performance preraks are found in the spheres of recreational and cultural activities, organisation of group discussions and participation of neo-literates in games and sports.

- The medium level performance of the preraks is found in the sphere of organisation of group discussions, running the library and reading room, conducting the sports and games. Providing information about developmental programmes and learning materials.
- The low level of performance of the preraks is found in the spheres library organisation, organising continuing education programmes and information centre, creation of educational environment, supply of inadequate sports materials and getting co-operation from the local cultural troops.
- There is a significant association between socio-economic and demographic characteristics of the preraks viz., sex, marital status, age, education and number of children and performance of the preraks.
- There is a significant relationship between sex, marital status, age, education and number of children and performance of the preraks.
- The intensity of the problems encountered by the preraks working in continuing education centres differs from group to group.
- The more prominent problems of the preraks is found in the sphere of collection of corpus fund, delay in receiving honorarium, non-availability of magazines, lack of audio-visual aids, lack of minimum facilities at the centres and men preraks organising the women neo-literates centres. Personal problems are lack of time, attending to other functions and lack of co-operation from the neo-literates.
- The prominent problems of the preraks are found in the sphere of agriculture work, family problems, financial problems, non co-operation of family

members and village educators, age difference between neo-literates and preraks, lack of experience, no rewards and awards to the preraks, lack of co-operation from the VAOs, VDOs, village elders and village leaders and non-supervision of the centres by the MPDOs.

- The less prominent problems of the preraks is found in the sphere of personal work, lack of qualifications, non-completion of primers, lack of co-operation from the Mandal literacy organizers, supervisors, continuing education centre chairman, sarpanch, ward members lack of teaching-learning materials and inadequate training of the preraks.
- Out of 120 preraks, one third (38) of the preraks are found to be facing more prominent problems, 42 per cent (50) of the preraks are found to be facing at prominent problems, one fourth (32) of the preraks is facing at less prominent problems.
- The preraks are of the opinion that personal problems are found to be more acute than the programme related problems.
- There is a significant association with type of family of the preraks and their personal problems. There is significant relationship between sex, marital status, education and number of children of the preraks and their personal problems.
- There is a close association between sex, marital status, age, caste, occupation, number of children and type of family of the preraks and their programme related problems. Further, it is also found that there is significant difference among the sex, age, caste and type of family of the preraks and their programme related problems.
- There is significant association between the sex, marital status and education of the preraks and their problems. There is significant difference

between the sex, education, number of children and their problems.

- The level of performance of the neo-literates attending in continuing education centres differs from group to group.
- 54 per cent of neo-literates have reached National Literacy Mission norm of high level performance, 40 per cent of the neo-literates are at medium level performance and remaining 6 per cent of the sample are at low level performance.
- There is close association between age and occupation and the performance of neo-literates. There is significant relationship among the sex, age and occupation of the neo-literates and their performance.
- The more prominent problems of the neo-literates are found in the sphere of organisation on the centre, inefficiency of teaching, lack of books, non-availability of library and reading room, lack of magazines, lack of self-employment opportunities, financial problems, heavy work, difficulty in dealing with 3Rs, shyness of women and child rearing duties of the women.
- The prominent problems of the neo-literates are found in the sphere of location on the centre at a distance, lack of minimum facilities, inadequate space at the centre, inconvenient timings, primers are difficult to learn, no separate centres for women, lack of quality of life improvement programmes, family problems, participation in agriculture work, lack of interest on education, lack of time, lack of unity among the neo-literates and non co-operation of the preraks.
- The less prominent problems of the neo-literates is found in the sphere of bad habits, poor health, migration to other places in search of work, lack

of co-operation from the family members, villagers and village leaders, equivalency programmes and individual interest promotion programmes are not organised at the centre.

- The intensity of the problems encountered by the neo-literates in attending the continuing education centres differs from group to group.
- There is a significant difference between the personal and programme related problems of the neo-literates.
- There is a significant association between the caste and income and the personal problems of the neo-literates. Further, it is also found that, there is a difference between income of the neo-literates and their personal problems.
- There is no significant association between neo-literates programme related problems and socio-economic and demographic characteristics viz., sex, marital status, age, caste, occupation, income, type of family and number of children.
- There is no significant association between neo-literates problems and their socio-economic and demographic characteristics viz., sex, marital status, age, caste, occupation, income, type of family and number of children.
- Positive opinion of the community representatives on the performance of preraks is found in the sphere of organising literacy awareness programmes, creation of awareness about self-help groups, organising group discussions, organisation of programmes related to literacy and development, maintaining records and registers and collection of corpus fund through village education committees.
- Negative opinion of the community representatives on the performance of preraks is poor on issues

related to provision of minimum facilities, supply of magazines, arranging audio-visual aids, lack of library and reading facilities, organisation of continuing education programmes, lack of cultural programmes in the centre, lack of teaching-learning materials, collection of information on developmental programmes and conducting sports and games in the centre.

- 44 per cent of the community representatives opined that the preraks performance was good in all aspects of continuing education centres. On the other hand, 56 per cent of the community representatives have negative opinion about the capacity of the preraks.
- There is a significant difference between the preraks performance and neo-literates performance.
- There is a significant difference between the preraks problems and neo-literate problems.
- There is a significant difference between the preraks performance and community opinion.

SUGGESTIONS FOR FURTHER RESEARCH

- Similar study can be undertaken with a large sample of preraks and neo-literates with more number of variables affecting their performance.
- A similar study can be taken on performance of other functionaries like nodal preraks and mandal literacy organisers with regard to their performance.
- A status of the impact of the training on the performance of the preraks can also taken up.
- In depth studies touching upon policy implications, materials and administration may be attempted.

IMPLICATIONS OF THE STUDY

The continuing education programme is planned meticulously with the Lansdale objectives of providing scope for neo-literates for retaining the skills, application of skills in day to day life and towards improving their quality of life. It is necessary to know the extent to which the preraks are performing their functions, the problems involved, the opinion of the community about the preraks and the activities of the continuing education centres, the performance of neo-literates and the problems of neo-literates in order to take up remedial measures. Though the guidelines and methodology suggested for implementing the programme remain constant throughout the country, the operationalisation of the programme is likely to differ at the gross root level depending upon the social-economic status and other issues. Studies of this nature are likely to prove useful to the district in particular when the evaluation work is carried out and to think about the ways and means of utilising the edgovers of evaluation to other districts.

The functions of the preraks are wide and varied and out of 45 items identified, the preraks of the study were found to be good at only 13 items and it was neither medium nor low with regard to the remaining 32 items which requires attention of the administration. The items pertaining to the medium level of performance are supply of daily newspapers, fortnightly and monthly magazines to the centre, conducting sports and games competitions, collection of corpus fund through village education committees, facilitating neo-literate participation in group discussion, creating awareness about programmes like DWCRA, CMEY, TRYSEM and DEEPAM, evaluating the progress of the centre, providing minimum facilities to the neo-literates, discussion about individual and village issues, organising short-term training programmes (leadership qualities, right to vote, agriculture, embroidery and tailoring), improving literacy skills of neo-literates in the evening classes, running the library and reading room, collection of information about developmental programmes, identification of learning needs of the neo-literates and preparing a plan to meet these needs, organising continuing education programmes through village education committees, arranging audio-visual aids, discussion about individual development of the neo-literates, organising quality of life improvement programmes, making people aware of the importance of the games and sports to neo-literates.

The items of low level performance are running the information centre, collection of funds and books to organise the library, running the centre for six days in a week, collecting books related to social, scientific, art and history, organising the equivalency programmes, creating conducive educational environment in the centre, creating awareness about the utility of games and sports, keeping records in continuing education centres about literacy and illiteracy, organising cultural programmes with the help of local cultural troops, organising development activities, organising self-employment programmes, organising recreational activities, helping the self-help groups to acquire literacy, and organising vocational training programmes.

In the present study it was found that gender, marital status, age and education have significantly influenced the performance of the preraks. The trend of the results showed that women preraks performance was low and the district administration has to take steps to improve their performance. Based on the results of the study where better mean performance scores are obtained, it can be suggested that while selecting the preraks preference can be given to married, 25 years and above age group, Intermediate and above qualified and people representing rural background. While attempting to improve the status of the centres, it would worthy to consider the problem of preraks like collection of corpus fund, regular payment of preraks honorarium, provision of dailies, weeklies, fortnightly and monthly magazines to the centres, provision of equipment like television, radio, tape recorders to the centres, provision of basic facilities in the centre, reducing the functions of the preraks, securing community support for the programme. One of the important findings of the study is that out of 360 neo-literates only 195 neo-literates exhibited high performance in literacy skills. The district administration has to take steps to identify the neo-literates who are medium and poor so that, their literacy levels can be enhanced.

Community participation is crucial implementing the continuing education programme. It was observed in the present study that the community members expressed a low profile on issues like organising equivalency programmes, providing minimum facilities to the neo-literates, arranging cultural programmes with the help of local cultural troupes, organising quality of life improvement programmes, supplying daily newspapers, monthly and fortnightly magazines to the centre, discussion about the individual and village issues, identification the learning needs of the neo-literates and preparing a plan to meet these needs, motivating the neo-literates to participate in games and sports, creating conducive educational environment in the centre, collecting the information about development programmes, discussion about the population, family planning and pollution, collection of the funds and books to organise the library, organising self-employment programmes, keeping records in continuing education centres about literacy and illiteracy in the village, organising recreational activities, running the centre for six days in a week, organising continuing education centre programmes through the village education committees, teaching the importance of games and sports to neo-literates, running the library and reading room, conducting sports and games competitions, running the information centre, getting help from Mandal Literacy Organisers and supervisors in organising the continuing education centre activities, collection of books related to social, scientific, art and history, evaluating the progress of the centres, arranging audio-visual aids, making aware of the uses of the games and sports. The district administration has to take steps to enhance that participation of the community so that the programme can be made successful.

BIBLIOGRAPHY

Adilakshmi (1993): An Investigation into the Working Conditions of the Jana Shikshana Nilayams and Opinion of the Preraks towards Jana Shikshana Nilayams, Master Dissertation, S.P. Mahila University, Tirupati.

Adinarayana Reddy, P. (1999): Post-Literacy and Continuing Education, Discovery Publishing House, 4831/24, Ansari Road, Prahlad Street, Daryaganj, New Delhi 110 002.

Asha. P.P. (2001): Role of SRC in Training Functionaries in Continuing Education Programme, Diploma in Non-formal Education, Centre for Adult, Continuing Education and Extension, Kariavattam Campus, University of Kerala, Thiruvananthapuram.

Creations (1996): Directorate of Adult Education, MHRD, Dept. of Education, Govt. of India, Block No.10, Jamnagar House Hutments, Shahjahan Road, New Delhi 110 011.

Denzil Saldana (1992): Evaluation of Total Literacy Campaign of Warda District, Bombay: TISS.

Deshpande & Indian Institute of Education (1993): Evaluation of Literacy Campaign, Jalna, Pune: State Resource Centre.

Dinesh Babu (1996): Instructor's Involvement in Continuing Education Programmes—At Kulathupuzha Panchayat, Diploma in Non-Formal Education, Centre for Adult, Continuing Education and Extension, Karaivattam Campus, University of Kerala, Thiruvananthapuram.

Directorate of Adult Education (1994): A Report of the Functioning of Jana Shikshan Nilayams, 1993-94, New Delhi: Govt. of India.

Directorate of Adult Education (1998): Scheme of Continuing Education for Neo-Literates by National Literacy Mission, Ministry of Human Resource Development, Dept. of Education, Govt. of India, Block No. 10, Jamnagar House Hutments, Shahjahan Road, New Delhi 110 011.

Directorate of Adult Education (1998); Towards a Literate India, National Literacy Mission, Ministry of Human Resource Development, Dept. of Education, Govt. of India, Block No.10, Jamnagar House Hutments, Shahjahan Road, New Delhi 110 011.

Directorate of Adult Education (2000); National Literacy Mission, Ministry of Human Resource Development, Dept. of Education, Govt. of India, Block No. 10, Jamnagar House Hutments, Shahjahan Road, New Delhi 110 011.

Directorate of Adult Education (2000); A Hand Book for Preraks, Ministry of Human Resource Development, Dept. of Education, Govt. of India, Block No. 10, Jamnagar House Hutments, Shahjahan Road, New Delhi 110 011.

Education for All (2000); National Institute of Adult Education, 10-B, Indra Prastha Estate, New Delhi.

Gireesan, K. (2000); Role of Local Government Institutions in the Implementation of CEPs in Kerala, Indian Journal of Adult Education, Vol. 61, No. 3, (July-Sept.)-2000, pp. 23 to 33.

Gokul O. Parek (1994); Evaluation of Literacy Campaign of Vadodara District, Ahmedabad, Sardar Patel Institute of Economic and Social Change.

Gupta, S.C. (1981); Fundamentals of Statistics, Himalaya Publishing House, Ramdoot, Dr.Bhalerao Marg, Girgaon, Mumbai–400 004.

Harsing Chouhan (2001); Problems of Post-Literacy Campaign: Causes and Remedies, Indian Journal of Adult Education, Vol. 62, No. 2, (April-June) 2001, pp. 37 to 42.

Indra Deva and Raja Sekhar (1993); Evaluation of Literacy Campaign, Bilaspur, Madhya Pradesh. Cited in Evaluation of Literacy Campaign: Summary Reports, Government of India.

Jagannada Rao, D. (2002); The Problems faced by Neo-Literates to attend Continuing Education Centres in Tirupati Rural Mandal of Chittoor District. M.A. Dissertation, S.V. University, Tirupati.

Janardhana Rao, V. (1996); An Enquiry in to the Problems faced by the Monitors in Jana Chaitanya Kendras, M.Phil. Thesis, S.V. University, Tirupati.

Janardhana Rao, V. (2002); A Study on the Problems and Performance of the Volunteers in 100-day Literacy Programme of Chittoor District, Ph.D. Thesis, S.V. University, Tirupati.

Jaya Kumar, V.S. (1996); Involvement of Akshara Sangham Conveners in Continuing Education Programme in Nemon

Panchayat, Diploma in Non-Formal Education, Centre for Adult, Continuing Education and Extension, Kariavattam Campus, University of Kerala, Thiruvananthapuram.

John, W. Best (1982); Research in Education, Prentice Hall of India Private Limited, M-97, Connaught Circus, New Delhi 110 001.

Kishore Attover (1994); Evaluation of Literacy Campaign, Shimoga District, Bangalore: School of Social Work.

Krishna Murthy and Others (1993); Evaluation of the TLC, Chittoor District, A Report, Hyderabad: The University of Hyderabad.

Krishna Murthy (2003); A Study on the Performance of Preraks in Anantapur District, M.A. Dissertation, Dept. of Adult Education, S.V. University, Tirupati.

Kumaraswamy. T., Bharathi, K.G. and Robert Dev Doss (2000); Influence of Training, Materials and Community Support on the Performance of Preraks Organising Continuing Education Centres, Indian Journal of Adult Education, Vol. 61, No. 3, pp. 52 to 60.

Krishna Swamy, O.R. (1993); Methodology of Research in Social Sciences, Himalaya Publishing House, Ramdoot, Dr. Bhalerao Marg, Girgaon, Mumbai 400 004.

Kusum Vir (1999); Present Status of Continuing Education, Indian Journal of Adult Education.

Kusum Vir (2000); The role of Preraks in Continuing Education Programme, Indian Journal of Adult Education, Vol. 61, No. 3 (July-Sept.), pp. 42-51.

Madan Singh (1999); Companion to Adult Educators, Published by National Literacy Mission, Ministry of Human Resource Development. Dept. of Education, Govt. of India, Block No. 10, Jamnagar House Hutments, Shahjahan Road, New Delhi 110 011.

Misra (1994); Evaluation of Literacy Campaign, Vikram University, Ratlam, Madhya Pradesh. Cited in Evaluation of Literacy Campaign: Summary Report, Government of India.

Mohanty and Prusty (1996); A Study of the Problems of Functioning of Jana Shikshana Nilayams, Indian Journal of Adult Education, Vol. 57(2), (April-June), pp. 46-51.

Muhammed Arif Khan (1996); Possibilities of Implementing Continuing Education Programme among Fisher Folk in Vizhinjam Panchayat, Post Masters Diploma in Adult,

Continuing Education and Extension, Kariavattam Campus, University of Kerala, Thiruvananthapuram.

Musthaqu Ahmad (1994): Evaluation of the TLC in Almora, Lucknow: State Resource Centre.

Muthuchamy (1992): A Study of the Role Performance of the Preraks, M.Phil. Dissertation, Alagappa University, Karaikudi.

Nair, Omanna and Rahim (1992): A Study of the Programmes and Activities of JSN organised by Nehru Yuva Kendra in Kerala, Thiruvananthapuram: Kerala Association for Non-Formal Education and Development.

NIRD (1994): Evaluation of Literacy Campaign, Chittoor District, A.P., Hyderabad, NIRD.

Padmanabhaiah and Kumaraswamy (1995): An Identification of the Problems faced by the Monitors, Indian Journal of Adult Education, Vol. 50(2), (April-June), pp. 42-46.

Prabhakar Reddy. N. (2000): A Study Report on the Root Causes of Low Strength in Continuing Education Centres, M.A., Dissertation, Dept. of Adult and Continuing Education, S.V. University, Tirupati.

Prem Chand (2000): Continuing Education Programme in South India: Problems and Prospects, Indian Journal of Adult Education, Vol. 61, No. 3, (July-Sept.), pp. 8-22.

Prem Chand and Others (1993): Evaluation of Literacy Campaign, Dungarpur, Rajasthan. Cited in Evaluation of Literacy Campaign: Summary Reports, NLM, Government of India, New Delhi.

Pushpavally. S. (1990): Needs and Problems of Adult in Mudavamughal Colony with special reference to Adult and Continuing Education, Centre for Adult, Continuing Education and Extension, Kariavattam, University of Kerala, Thiruvananthapuram.

Rahi, A.L. (1996): Adult Education Policies and Programmes, the Associated Publishers, 2963/2, Kacha Bazar, Plot No.56, Ambala Cantt 133 001, India.

Raja Rao, D. (1999): A Study of Jana Shikshan Nilayam in Visakhapatnam District, A.P., Ph.D. Thesis, Dept. of Adult and Continuing Education, Andhra University, Visakhapatnam.

Rani, R. (1992): A Study on the Involvement of Avinashilingam Deemed University, Coimbatore in the Adult/Continuing Education Programme.

Ranjinadoss. M.J.A. and Anita Machado (1998); A Study on Needs and Interest of Neo-Literates with Reference to Continuing Education Books to be Developed, Literacy Mission, Vision Indian Charitable Trust, 16, Aditya Sadan, Ashoka Road, Phase-II, New Delhi, Vol. XXIII/No. 16.

Reddeppa (1994): A Study of the Determinants of Prerak Effectiveness, M.Phil. Thesis, S.V.University, Tirupati.

Rokadia (1993): Evaluation of Literacy Campaign, Ajmir, Rajasthan. Cited in Evaluation of Literacy Campaign: Summary Reports, NLM, Government of India, New Delhi.

Sandeep P. and Madhumathi, C. (1999): Non-formal Adult and Continuing Education: Insights for 21st Century, Veera Educational Services and Consultancy Pvt. Ltd., 12-13-677-12, Kimtee Colony, Tarnaka, Secunderabad 500 017.

Santhosh Alias (2000): A Continuing Model based on the Contributions of EMS for Social uplift, Diploma in Non-Formal Education, Centre for Adult, Continuing Education and Extension, Kariavattam Campus, University of Kerala, Thiruvananthapuram.

Sardar Patel Institute of Economic and Social Research (1993): Evaluation of Literacy, Kheda District, Ahmedabad: SPIESR.

Sardar Patel Institute of Economic and Social Research (1994): Evaluation of Literacy Campaign of Dang District, Ahmedabad: SPIESR.

Sardar Patel Institute of Economic and Social Research (1994): Evaluation of Literacy Campaign of Sundar Nagar District, Ahmedabad: SPIESR.

Sidday Gowda, Y.S. (1996): Aksharavani, External Evaluation Report of TLC, Chitradurga District, Karnataka, Mysore University.

Soundarapandian, M. (1994): Socio-economic Status of Volunteer Instructors and Drop-out Learners of Total Literacy Campaign, Indian Journal of Adult Education, Vol. 55, No. 3, pp. 23-31.

State Resource Centre (1995): An Observational Study to Identify the Role of JSN in Continuing Education, SRC, Mysore

State Resource Centre; Continuing Education Programme, Training Modules, Hyderabad: SRC.

Sudha Rani and Surendra (2001): Continuing Education—A Vehicle for Community Development, Social Welfare Journal, Vol.48, No.4, (July), 2001, pp. 16-17.

Surya Prakasham, G. (2000): An Enquiry into the Problems of Preraks of Continuing Education Centres in Tirupati Revenue

Division, M.A., Dissertation, Dept. of Adult and Continuing Education, S.V.University, Tirupati.

Syam, A. and Bhaskaracharyulu, Y. (1999): Evaluation Report of Continuing Education Centres: Srikakulam District, Dept. of Adult and Continuing Education, Andhra University, Visakhapatnam.

Tata Institute of Social Science (1993): Evaluation of TLC in Nanded, Bombay: TISS.

Tata Institute of Social Science (1993): Evaluation of TLC in Lathur, Bombay: TISS.

Vasantha Kumari, Sudha Rani and Uma Devi (2000): The Problems faced by Neo-literates in attending Continuing Education Centres, Indian Journal of Adult Education, Vol. 61, No. 3 (July-Sept.), pp. 61-70.

Vasantha Kumari, P., Sampoornam, R. and Venkata Lakshumma, G. (2002): Problems faced by Volunteers in Attending Akshara Sankranti Programme, Journal of Adult Education and Development, Vol. 15, No. 4-6 (July-Dec.), pp. 3-6.

Vasantha Kumari, P., Sudha Rani and Surendra, G. (2002): Continuing Education Programme—A Study of Constraints, Indian Journal of Adult Education, Vol. 63, No. 3 (July-Sept.), pp. 34-38.

Vasudeva Rao, B.S. (1996): Evaluation of Total Literacy Campaign in Nellore district, Dept. of Adult and Continuing Education, Andhra University, Visakhapatnam.

Vasumathi (1992): A Study of the Organisation and Functions of Jana Shikshana Nilayams under Area Development Approach of the NLM in the Colleges of Kannur District, Master Dissertation, Calicut University, Calicut, Kerala.

Vengaiah, S. (2001): Continuing Education Needs of the Tribal Women in Chittoor District of A.P., M.Phil. Thesis, Dept. of Adult and Continuing Education, S.V. University, Tirupati.

Visions (1995): Directorate of Adult Education, MHRD, Dept. of Education, Govt. of India, Block No.10, Jamnagar House Hutments, Shahjahan Road, New Delhi 110 011.

Viswanadha Gupta, P. & Janardhana Reddy, D. (2000): A Study on the Functioning of Continuing Education Centres in Chittoor District, Indian Journal of Adult Education, Vol. 61, No. 3 (July-Sept.), pp. 34-41.

William, J. Goode and Paul, K. Hatt (1952): McGraw Hill Kogakeioha Ltd., New Delhi.

Index